TREET
& TERRACES

A BYGONE ERA OF

NEW TOWN
UPPER NORWOOD SE19

BERYL D. CHEESEMAN

THEBAN PUBLISHING
DORMANSLAND • SURREY

BERYL D CHEESEMAN
33 BEACON HILL
DORMANSLAND
SURREY RH7 6RQ
TEL: 0342-832585

Published by
Theban Publishing
33 Beacon Hill,
Dormansland
Surrey
RH7 6RQ

ISBN 0-9518803-0-6

Cover illustrations
Front: Hermitage Road
Back: Rear of New Town.

Designed and produced by Words & Images,
2 Charlton Cottages, Barden Road, Speldhurst, Tunbridge Wells, Kent TN3 0LH
Printed in Great Britain by Antony Rowe Ltd, Chippenham, Wiltshire

Dedicated to My Mum.
For all her past memories.

Ancestral voices obscured from view,
Each generation starting anew,
Searching archives, forever to find,
Our past, our heritage of those behind.

ACKNOWLEDGMENTS

I would like to thank the following people for the help and assistance that was given to me in my research of New Town;

Mr. Horace Margets for his many memories: Mrs. Joan Warwick for her help and valued assistance; Mr. Charles Smith; Mr. Leonard Whiteman; Mrs. Guy Johnson; and Mrs. C. Palmer for their antidotes on New Town life; my cousin Miss Pamela Rice assisting with photographs; plus my ever suffering husband and all my relatives and friends for their encouragement and enthusiasm in helping me to try and capture a little of the past, in this very small part of Norwood.

Illustrations by Mrs. Jacqueline Sinclair.

Acknowledgments also to:
Mr. Steven Roud, Croydon Local Studies,
who was the first to instigate my investigation
The Upper Norwood Library
Minet Archives
Whitgift Archives
Anerley Library
South Norwood Library
Spurgeons College
Mrs. Susan Mills of the Baptist Union, Regents Park College.

Books consulted :
Memories of Norwood since 1852   Mrs. Elizabeth Dee
A Social & Economic History of England 1700-1970   A.H. Stamp
British Economic & Social History 1700-1982   C.W. Munn
Croydon –The Great War   Moore & Sayers
Pastor & Guardian   John Stuart
The Story of Norwood   J.B. Wilson
The Phoenix Suburb   Alan J. Warwick
The Candlestick and The Torch   Mr. Curruthers
Norwood Review & The Norwood News
Plus many small articles in pamphlets.

CONTENTS

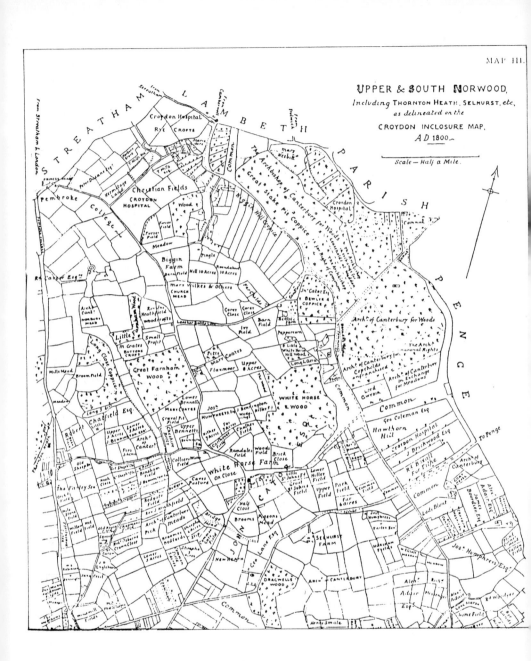

PLATE 1
Croydon Inclosure Map 1800

6

1854 Penge Palace, Upper Norwood – the new location for the Crystal Palace transferred from Hyde Park, London. Change followed very quickly from the once rural quiet countryside to a very desirable residential, expanding area. Hotels, railway stations and property opened up a new life and environment to the small Victorian population.

The main route from the Crystal Palace to Streatham saw at this time several established houses standing in what is now Oxford Road, more were added and in course of time a 'New Town' came to be established. Gradually high walls were erected all round the area causing dismay to the local inhabitants, but slowly and gradually a community spirit grew within the walls with each passing generation.

Mainly, this book is based on the social conditions at the end of the nineteenth century and the first two decades of the twentieth century, ending when the controversial enclosing wall was finally demolished about 1930.

The printed history of towns and places provide a general link with the past. Rarely are mentioned the day to day events which shaped the lives of ordinary men, women and children. These people lived and died without notoriety and with the passage of time are often forgotten.

I do not profess to have any prior literary experience and can only justify myself in writing this brief history by saying that I am descended from four generations who lived in New Town. Many memories have been passed on to me by my mother, relations and older aquaintances and to these are added mine having lived there as a small child.

Generally people remember past events quite differently, but it is hoped that somewhere between these pages a little of the atmosphere of New Town in that early period has been captured.

Convent and Orphanage, Central Hill.

All Saints, Upper Norwood Parish Church.

CHAPTER ONE

NEW TOWN

Norwood – once part of the Great North Wood, the name derived from 'being the wood that lay to the North of Croydon'. Set amidst hills, woodland and common, the air was said to be pure because of the extensive height.

Various old farmsteads and cottages were scattered about with well worn tracks winding their way through the woods and copses. In ancient times the land called Gravelly Hill Coppice covered most of the area where New Town lay, and further south The Great Steak Pit Coppice.

There were many enclosure acts but the real development of the district began with the Croydon Enclosure Act of 1800.

In the year 1797 an Act of Parliament was passed to enclose the waste lands of Croydon, which then became enfranchised, or rendered freehold property, and the Archbishop of Canterbury granted leases for building.

Norwood by 1850 grew out of all proportion as labourers ventured in from the neighbouring areas for employment with the Crystal Palace. New Town has nothing to boast of in the way of ancient history, it was just a parcel of land, earmarked as a building plot.

Adjacent to the west, stood the Park Hotel, owned by Mr. Crawley, formerly the home of the celebrated Mrs. Mary Nesbitt. By 1847 the property had been acquired by a religious community from France and called the Monastery de la Notre Dame des Orphelins of Normandy, until finally in 1850 it became known as Virgo Fidelis, the Catholic Convent. The convent was surrounded by large oaks bearing new growth and young trees season after season, one of the last vintage sites remaining that had once been part of the great North Wood.

On the other side to the east saw a fine house known as Essex Lodge, later called The Truscott Estate, the landscaped gardens and ornamental ponds now covered by Rockmount Road.

Between the above, the New Town land lay on waste land sloping down from the lower part of Central Hill, called Central Valley. At the lowest point was a small stream, then from there, fields rose up again towards Church Road & Beulah Hill. The landscape of beautiful valleys and hills, viewed from this height, must surely have looked a picturesque panorama.

Near to the small stream, and either side of a tree lined narrow track, stood two giant oak trees. At a later date this track became known as an 'Undeclared public highway,' eventually to be called Hermitage Road. In 1934 when the development began outside New Town, one of the oak trees

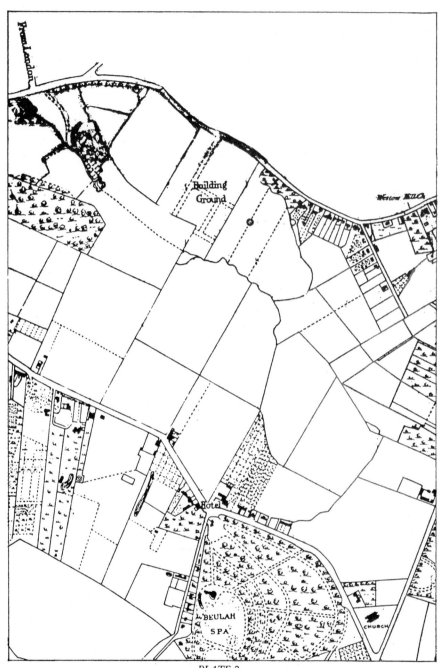

PLATE 2
New Town building land, 1840.

10

was demolished, leaving one solitary oak tree standing, a reminiscence of a bygone age. It stands there still, viewing the many changes that have taken place.

Earlier conveyances show that the New Town land was originally part of the Biggin Hill Farm estate. 1846 saw the break up of Biggin Hill Farm and various lots were for sale. Lot 7, 9a 0r 38p (9acres 0 rods 38 perches), was the size of New Town acreage.

At this period there seems to be some confusion between Central Hill and Oxford Road, in most cases they seem to be classed as one. There are mentions of Central Hill being formerly Gravel Hill, formerly Westward Road and the same applied to Oxford Road.

1847 Mr. Henry Gillingham leased land at the top of Oxford Road for 99 years from Mr. John Roper. Six houses were built and in 1865 two more houses erected.

1849 Mr. Samuel Clapham built five cottages called Prospect Place. Oxford Road. The Clapham family kept connections with New Town well into the twentieth century, weekly rents still being collected from these small cottages.

At the bottom of the hill, which is now Crystal Terrace, some of the land was owned by Mr. Nash, and this description is one of the few found that mentions the ditch;

N/W partly by road, late of Mr. Nash, S/W by a ditch, adjoining nunnery grounds.

The ordinance survey maps show the river Effra as running alongside Chevening Road and then emerging underground. The ditch is shown on a small scale map as being close to New Town, maybe a tributary of the river Effra. There was suggestion of a proposed road running between Crystal Terrace and Eagle Hill but this did not materialise. Instead, a mission hall was built, described in the directories as an Iron Church. Mrs. Elizabeth Louisa Dee's valued account of New Town in her book *Memories of Norwood since 1852* give the earliest description of New Town and a small sketch of the first houses. *(See page 12).*

These are a few extracts from her book:

New Town appeared as if by magic. We lived at the top of Oxford Road, behind us was a field called 'Billy Woods Field' and further on the Convent woods. Our house was called Harmony House, it was approached by steps at the side and a nice porch of trellis work, covered with creeping flowers, it contained five rooms and scullery with a pump in it. A good long garden and a large shed, sometimes we had to fetch water from the well when the pump was dry, we also had a large rain butt for catching rain water for washing.

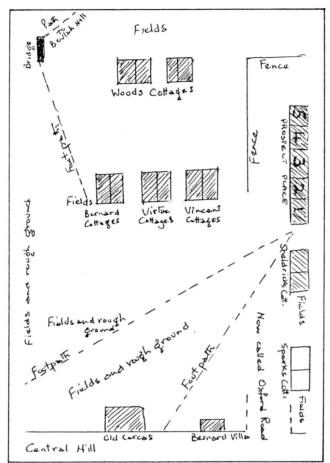

Fields

Path to Beulah Hill

Bridge

Fence

Fence

PROSPECT PLACE

Woods Cottages

Fields

Fields

Bernard Cottages

Virtue Cottages

Vincent Cottages

Fields and rough ground

Fields and rough ground

Footpath

Fields and rough ground

Footpath

Now called Oxford Road

Sparks Cott.

Sparks Cott.

Fields

Fields

Fields

Central Hill

Old Carcos

Bernard Villa

PLATE 3
Mrs. Dee's plan
of New Town, 1852

The freehold fields of Mr. Clapham were situated where Crystal Terrace now stands. My uncle Mr. Maidman built Crystal Terrace, he died in 1862 and the property was sold to Mr. Warren, the butcher in Westow Street. My father prepared the plans, and the water was first brought into New Town for Crystal Terrace at my father's instigation.

Fields went right down to what is now called Eagle Hill, then you came to a little path on the right, here were four cottages, called Woods Cottages, to the left two pieces of ground one of which Mr. Street rented and the other Mr. Dee who used them for vegetable growing, when Mr. Dee left Norwood, Mr. Street had both of them and later built two houses on the ground. By the side of the ground was what was called a bridge over the river Effra, practically it consisted of about four planks across a wide ditch, but still it was the bed of the Effra.

12

The earliest mention of New Town officially recorded is in the *Croydon Directory* of 1855:

Sarah Robinson   Grocer
Joseph Chamberlain   Beer Retailer

The *Croydon Directory* of 1859 lists the previous shops, plus:

Mr. J. King   Baker
Mr. James   North Butcher
Mr. Isaac Smith   Publican The Eagle

By 1864 there was a sharp increase in various traders:

Ephraim Grant   Grocer
Richard Wheatley   Baker
Benjamin Bloom   Grocer
Wm. Pitcher   Butcher
Henry Robinson   Grocer
John Ticehurst   Coffee Shop
S. Cooper   Bootmaker
Mr. Clapham   Bootmaker
D. Salmon   Bootmaker
Wm. Abnett   Beer Retailer
Isaac Smith   Eagle Tavern
Lawrence Fahey   Boot & Shoe repair
Edward Taylor   Cab & Fly Proprietor

Information gleaned from the Croydon Rate books relative to the early period shows that frequently many of the houses were constructed by small local builders, who each built several houses then proceeded to live in one, drawing rents from the remainder. The majority of printed records give reference to the fact that New Town was built to house the Irish labourers and navvies who were employed in the building of the Crystal Palace. Research shows that the Crystal Palace was completed in 1854, and the main buildings in New Town were not completed until much later.

The 1861 census returns show many Irish people living in Upper Norwood, but for the area of New Town, only nine are shown of Irish descent, three of these being police constables employed by the Crystal Palace. A large number of lodgers were shown, their families presumably joining them at a later date, many from neighbouring counties and even beyond. Craftsmen of all descriptions were employed by the Crystal Palace – master carpenters, builders, glaziers, stone masons, and other skilled labourers and workers.

Throughout the earlier period there were access points to footpaths from Crystal Terrace, Albert Road, and New Spa Road, but at a later date the inhabitants lost the use of these openings by walls being erected. The walls were all at different levels, boundary walls at the ends of gardens were about 5-6' high, and walls across all openings were as high 10'-12'.

During the year 1859 there are many references to new houses in New Town, although it took many more years for the final buildings to be constructed. Development at the lower end of Eagle Hill was halted, because of the ditch or watercourse which ran across at the lowest point. Consequently, to enable the extra development, a culvert was built to take the watercourse beneath the road.

An extract taken from the minutes of the Croydon Local Board of Health in 1861-1864 states:

The tender of Mr. Hayward for draining the ditch with red pipes at Central Hill Norwood for £31 was accepted.

Several years later, with the formation of Rockmount School, the culvert was widened. There are many mentions about the watercourse in the Croydon Health minutes:

Mr. Langley reported as to the nuisance in South Vale, Norwood and suggested that the storm water which flowed over the road, should be conveyed through a covered drain into the watercourse, which should cost about £5.

In the rainy seasons the water would flow freely, yet at other times it would be well drained, and the children used this as their play area, jumping backwards and forwards across the open ditch. It was very much a part of the New Town scene. There are some amusing incidents about the 'ditch', one in particular related to me by Aunt Mary Terry. One of the boys was dared to crawl into the culvert, generally referred to as the 'red pipes'; he became stuck and the police were called to set the boy free.

During the second world war, Anderson shelters were erected in the gardens, and to the south of Hancock Road flooding often occurred in them. There were many comments from the older generation 'that this was where the ditch used to be'. Springs abound in the area and even to-day springs often emerge in the gardens of the neighbourhood. It was well known that the cellar of The Oxford Arms was cooled by the springs in the locality which contributed to the prime condition of the fine ales which were sold there.

Further reports from the Health Minutes, Years 1861-1864:

Mr. Howard attended and stated that the drainage of the houses in New Town Norwood was in a very bad state and the surveyor was directed to meet him and do what was necessary to remedy the effect.

Mr. Howard attended and complained that the nuisance caused by the imperfect draining at New Town, Norwood had not been given to Mr. Deacon the agent of the owner of the cottage to connect them with the public sewer and it was ordered that if the connections were not made by Thursday next, the surveyor should perform the work and charge the owner with the expenses.

This piece taken from the *Norwood News* gives an excellent description of just how the earlier New Town may have looked:

We understand that a memorial is in process of signature by the ratepayers and inhabitants of Norwood New Town, addressed to the Board of Health respecting the bad state of the roads in that locality. The step is not taken a moment too soon, for the condition of the so called thoroughfares could, we should suppose, hardly be parallelled in any other thickly populated and long established neighbourhood in the suburbs of London.

The main road from Central Hill, Oxford Road, presents a variegated aspect, the roadway being checquered with spaces of hard ground, alternating with patches of thick clayed mud, picturesque enough in its proper place in the backwoods of America, but quite out of character of a village of at least 1000 inhabitants.

The manifold and deeply indented ruts indicate numerous struggles for extrication on the part of the heavily laden vehicles, while rapidly undulating surface, now hill, now dale, must cause sensations to riders and drivers similar to those induced by the passage of the Channel in a heavy swell.

The first road to the left is simply a sea of mud; the second is better; its principal defect being the absence of distinction between carriageway and footway which seems to be characteristic of the roads under the paternal care of the Croydon Board. But the most crying evil is the state of Spa Road, if road it can be called, whose only claim to the name is that it has a row of houses on each side. In its best state its Alpine steepness renders it a Hill. Difficulty both for vehicles and asthmatic wayfarers; but in its present state it is [not] a sight for Gods and men.

Let not, however, the mortal visit it after daylight has departed. We have called it Alpine; that character is well supported not only by its steepness which renders it almost inaccessible to all but pedestrians, but by other features characteristic of a mountain district, such as its rugged surface and projecting stones, left bare by long absence of supersoil, and its ravine, in the shape of a deep trench, worn by the rapid torrent, which hurries down its declivity in rainy weather a trench deep enough to inflict serious injury on any unlucky passer who might miss his footing. Some enterprising and ingenious individual has, at one time or another attempted to supply the want of a curb by setting thin boards edgewise but this attempt has been abandoned in despair when half accomplished and for one half of the road all distinctions are obliterated. Add to this that there are no lamps, and our readers will agree with us that we are not exagerating when we say that it is not mearly unpleasant, but positively dangerous to attempt to traverse this road after daylight. Unless inhabitants are gifted with feline power of sight, or through long practice are thoroughly acquainted with every pitfall and quagmire that lies in the way, or unless they adopt at nightfall never venturing out after dark (which we do not think characteristic of New Town) we should imagine that broken limbs and sprained ankles are of daily occurrence in Spa Road.

Yet as we have intimated above, this is not a newly-built district, nor in an uninhabited place, but in a locality covered with houses and which has paid rates for many years, this latter point is the great grievance, for the inhabitants may well begin to question the justice of exacting highway rates at all, when they have no highways worthy of the name.

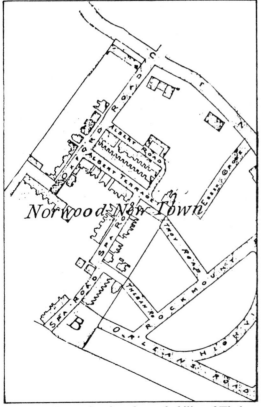

New Town showing the probability of Theban and Troy roads.

The amount of dwellings continued to rise quickly up by 1880:

1861 – 89 dwellings
1865 – 104 dwellings
1869 – 140 dwellings
1880 – 147 dwellings

There were many road changes and re-number-ings of the individual houses:

Naseby Road
    formerly Albert Terrace.

Dover Road
    formerly Albert Road
    formerly Truscott Place.

Eagle Hill
    formerly Spa New Road
    formerly Beulah Terrace.

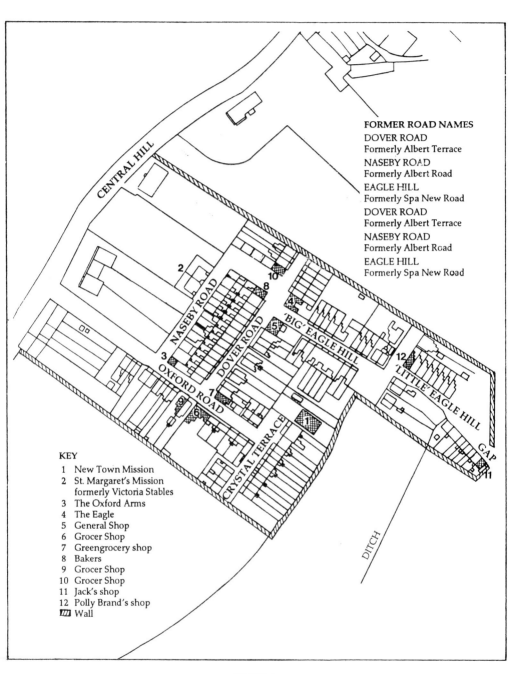

FORMER ROAD NAMES
DOVER ROAD
Formerly Albert Terrace
NASEBY ROAD
Formerly Albert Road
EAGLE HILL
Formerly Spa New Road
DOVER ROAD
Formerly Albert Terrace
NASEBY ROAD
Formerly Albert Road
EAGLE HILL
Formerly Spa New Road

KEY
1 New Town Mission
2 St. Margaret's Mission
   formerly Victoria Stables
3 The Oxford Arms
4 The Eagle
5 General Shop
6 Grocer Shop
7 Greengrocery shop
8 Bakers
9 Grocer Shop
10 Grocer Shop
11 Jack's shop
12 Polly Brand's shop
▨ Wall

PLATE 4
New Town 1895.

17

Top: left to right, Alf, Bob, Joe and Jim Townsend.
Above: George M. Mead, c1898. Son of George Mead master carpenter,
who was responsible for the construction of the pews in Virgo Fidelies.

Rev. C.H. Spurgeon preaching at the Crystal Palace.

NEW TOWN BAND OF HOPE.—A meeting in connection with the ninth anniversary of the Norwood New Town Band of Hope, was held on Monday evening in the Mission Room. The chair was occupied by Mr. W. Mitchell Carruthers, who read the report, from which it appeared that there were 215 children on the register, with an average monthly attendance of 69. The committee wished to tender their thanks to all who had assisted them during the year by addressing the children or in any way conducing to their improvement, and especially to those who gave such material assistance at the flower show, which was held on the August Bank Holiday, and which was the most successful that has ever taken place. Their thanks were also due to Mr. Everett for the fortnightly use of the Mission Room, and to all friends and subscribers. From the balance sheet we learn that the receipts for the general fund amounted to £16 15s. 1½d., and the expenditure to £13 8s. 7½d., leaving a balance in hand of £3 6s. 6d. The money received towards the flower show fund amounted to £42 19s. 6¼d., and the disbursements to £36 14s. 4d., leaving a balance in hand of £6 5s. 2¼d. The prizes were then distributed by Miss Horne to the following members:—Girls—equal first, Louisa Hill and Ellen Page; equal second, Lucy Page and Edith Hill. Boys—equal first, Nichol Weatherston and James Weatherston; equal second, Frederick Howard and Herbert Howard. Badges given to those who had attended no less than 15 meetings during the year: Harriett Howard, Lilian Kitchen, Elizabeth Mead, Henry Mead, Bertha Page, Emily Elphick, and Robert Reed. Medals for those who have belonged to the society for one year, and attended the meetings: Louisa Andrews, Louisa Dee, Edith Hill, Louisa Mead, Constance Johnson, Ellen Stanford, Rose Wood, Alice Stanford, Frank Martin, Bertie Cutting, Albert Starr, and Herbert Howard. Certificates to those who had been in the society three years and attended the meetings: Rosa Stevens, Ann Stanford, Robert Martin, Marshall Reed, Robert Reed, and William Ives. A service of song was performed by the choir and friends, taken from Hesba Stretton's well-known book, "Jessica's first Prayer." The solo parts were taken by the Misses Page, Packman, Willsmore, and Vincent. A vote of thanks was accorded to the chairman on the motion of Mr. Spens, and a similar compliment having been accorded to Mr. Battle, the director, those present separated.

NORWOOD NEW TOWN MISSION ROOM. — The Sunday school anniversary of this place of worship was celebrated on Sunday last, when three sermons were preached, in the morning by the Rev. George Rogers, senior tutor of the Rev. C. H. Spurgeon's Pastors' College; in the afternoon by the Rev. J. McCann, D.D., and in the evening by the Rev. E. T. Anderson, B.A., formerly an African slave, now of Regent's Park College. The services were all well attended, particularly that of the evening, when the room and lobby were crowded with an attentive congregation, and numbers were unable to obtain admittance. On Monday a tea took place, at which there were 150 present. This was followed by a public meeting, which was presided over by the Rev. Walter Hobbs, the much respected pastor. From the report read by Mr. G. Willoughby, the secretary, who has worked most zealously on behalf of the school, it appeared that the number of scholars on the books was 180, with a teaching staff of 25. The average attendance of scholars in the morning was 95, teachers 11; and in the afternoon 152, teachers 16; the largest attendance of scholars in the morning being 121, and in the afternoon 178. This showed a steady increase on the numbers of the previous year, and the school was never in a more hopeful condition than at the present time. The esteemed superintendent (Mr. Smith), who had laboured in the school for more than twelve years, was always most persevering in his efforts to promote the welfare of the scholars, and the committee hoped that he would be long spared to hold the post which he had so long and faithfully discharged. The various classes were all progressing favourably. The increase of the number of scholars had necessarily occasioned a larger outlay of money during the year, and the finances at present showed a small deficit. During the evening Rev. E. T. Anderson made a few very telling remarks, in the course of which he said he had been highly gratified by the manner in which the children had acquitted themselves in their recitations and singing that evening, and he thought it ought to encourage mothers to send their children to school, instead of allowing them to rove the streets. A lengthy programme, consisting of recitations and vocal music, was rendered by the scholars and teachers, and was greatly enjoyed. The following are the names of the children who took part:— Henry Menke, David Rockingham, Wm. Bryant, Charles Johnston, Geo. Cutting, Harry Raven, Jane Green, Rose Arnold, Harriet Howard, Bertha Page, Annie Rockingham, Emily Cutting, Alice Raven, Ada Philbrook, F. Ellis, Kate Chisen, Thos. Meade, Edwin Joyce, George Wells, Clara Starr, Rose Gibbs, Ellen Osborne, Alice Martin, Phœbe Martin, Thos. Bartlett, William Ottwell, Edward Osborne, J. McIver, Chas. Collins, George Howard, Maude Bartlett, Bertha Hobbs, and Amy Laud. At the conclusion of the programme, Mr. Searle moved a vote of thanks to the children and teachers for the manner in which they had entertained them that evening, which, on being put, was carried amidst applause. The chairman said there was one thing which they wanted in New Town, and that was a Coffee Palace, where the working men could go and read the paper at night without getting their brains muddled. (Cheers.) Mr. Searle had already promised his help, and he, (the chairman), trusted that others would come forward, and then he hoped before very long they would have this boon which was sadly needed.

Rev. Walter Hobbs.

ST. ANDREW'S MISSION CHURCH, NEWTOWN

The first anniversary of Mr. Gage at Newtown was held last Sunday and Monday. The morning service was conducted by Mr. Wm. Carruthers, F.R.S., Pd.D. who preached a simple discourse on the love of God, which was greatly appreciated. Mr. Gage conducted the evening service and spoke upon "A Working Church."

On Monday evening the Rev. J. M. Witherow, M.A., presided over a large and enthusiastic social gathering. Refreshments were arranged by Miss E. R. Blomfield and Miss Torr Jennings, assisted by a number of friends.

Letters of regret for absence were received from Sir C. E. Tritton, Bart., Rev. Martin Ansley, M.A., B.D., of the London City Mission, Rev. A. T. Kinnings, Mr. Wm. Carruthers, F.R.S., Mr. and Mrs. Clark, and others.

After a few words of hearty congratulation to the Newtown workers, Mr. Witherow on behalf of the Mission Council and friends presented Mr. Gage with a cheque as a token of their warm appreciation of the work being done.

The speakers were Messrs. J. Stone Blomfield, H. S. P. Hindley, H. B. Milne, F. H. A. Wedekind, C. E. Baldwin and A. Spong. All spoke of the encouraging character of the work carried on.

Mr. Gage briefly thanked the friends for their cheering messages and their generous gift.

The singing of Miss Gibson, Mrs. Hindley, Miss E. Penny and the choir was greatly enjoyed, and at the close an expression of thanks was given to all who had contributed to the success of the anniversary gatherings.

CHAPTER TWO

THE TWO MISSIONS

References to the New Town mission start to appear in the local newspapers about 1870 although no records could be found as to who actually owned the mission. The mission was located in the east corner of Crystal Terrace. It lay on a slope, and the entrance to the mission was through two iron gates, to the side of which, steps ran down to the lower rooms which were used for other functions.

Before the building of Rockmount School, lessons were held here and I can remember very high desks and forms. The Baptist handbook of 1869-1870 called the mission 'New Town Union Church' – Pastor John Batey 1870-1873.

It has been recorded that in the year 1877 Mr. E.J. Everett, at his own cost, purchased the mission for £3000 on the understanding that the church would be open to all denominations. In two references found of Mr. E.J. Everett, one said that he was of the Plymouth Brethren and the other that he was a Paedo Baptist.

The well known Baptist Minister C.H Spurgeon, was in some way connected with the 'Iron Church', a report of his funeral at West Norwood Cemetery in 1892 stated 'that the teachers and Sunday school of New Town, lined the entrance to the cemetery gates'. The Rev. C.H. Spurgeon was very popular with all working classes, and was a regular visitor on their door steps.

The Rev. Walter Hobbs was a student at Charles Haddon Spurgeon Pastor College and was requested by Mr. E.J. Everett to preach the Sunday Sermon at New Town mission. This was an honour for the community of New Town to hear one of the first sermons by the Rev. Walter Hobbs, and as his popularity grew he was asked to become pastor in 1878.

This is an extract taken from the *Baptist Handbook*:

Mr Hobbs' sermon on the first day consisted of eleven persons. He continued there throughout his college course, and the building had soon to be enlarged at the cost of £1000. Finally, he settled as pastor and remained until 1880, by which time the membership had increased to 180. Mr Hobbs was, however, a Baptist by conviction, and this led to his leaving the mission and accepting an invitation from a small community of Baptists meeting in Paxton Schoolroom, Norwood, (the beginning of the Baptist Church in Gipsy Road).

No minister could have been more conscientious, or more liked and appreciated than the Rev. Walter Hobbs. An extract taken from the *Crystal Palace District Times* states:

Rev. Hobbs had throughout shown, not only a brotherly unselfish and generous spirit, but the spirit of a minister of the gospel and true Christian.

He loved children and organised the bread and milk breakfasts for the poor children when he was a minister at Gipsy Road Baptist Church. The majority of marches for the unemployed were led by the Rev. Walter Hobbs.

During the first year of his pastorship at Gipsy Road Baptist Church, the Rev. Hobbs was one of the organisers of a great Temperance mission held in Norwood in March 1881.

The Temperance Society held many of their meetings in the mission, as did also The Band of Hope:

1886 January 9th Temperance meeting New Town. Vocal and instrumental music and recitations by the following members: Messrs. Buttle, Geary, Deacon, Gibbs, Page, Howard, Vincent. Three pledges were taken and eleven ribbons donned.

1886 March 27th New Town Band of Hope – 10th Anniversary last Monday 217 names on register – 30 new members and ten left.

1887 July 10th New Town Gospel Temperance Society, Mr. Canham Treasurer. Mr. Buttle Choir.

1887 Aug 6th Norwood Flower Show – Division 1 – open to members of Sunday Schools and Band of Hope. Edward Jones & Harriet Jones. New Town.

The mission was used for all kinds of functions. There were Sunday morning prayer and evening services; Fellowship meetings; Mothers' meetings; (a firm favourite with the women of New Town, where otherwise would they hear of the local gossip?!); lantern slide evenings and a Men's club. Open air meetings were held regularly in the summer on the Norwood Recreation ground. 1899 saw the start of the Girls Guild, and later the Boys Brigade. This must have closed, and the Boys Brigade restarted at a later date, as there is mention of them being presented with colours in 1927 and 1928, when Mr. Fred Mason ran a successful Brigade troop. The smart brigade would parade outside the mission, then march through New Town banging drums and blowing bugles.

Various competitions were arranged for the children of the Sunday schools, the mission feeling very proud of those who succeeded in obtaining recognition.

1887 March 19th Upper Norwood Industrial Exhibition. Prizes given to many children amongst them; Harriet Howard, New Town 3rd prize 2/6d for needlework in flannel or cloth. Crewel: Annie Howard 2nd prize 5/-.

1887 Scriptural examinations for prizes of Norwood & Penge Auxilliam Sunday School Union. Harriet Howard, New Town Mission Second Class certificate. William Rockingham & Kate Howard New Town.

By 1896 the mission was in financial difficulties, and St. Andrews Congregational Church, Westow Street, was approached with a request for aid and assistance. A legacy of £300 had been left by Mr. Everett, but this was soon exhausted, and the trustees offered the building to St Andrews Congregational Church for 1/- per year.

In 1900 it was resolved that it would be more desirable to organise the mission on Presbyterian lines, and a conference with the trustees was arranged. After months of tedious negotiations, St. Andrews Congregational Church at last purchased the property of New Town mission hall for £480, plus £200 to be spent on repairs. A mission council was constituted in 1906 with a minister of St. Andrews as president.

Miss Mackenzie formed a junior temperance choir. The well appreciated soup kitchens were organised in the winter, and these occupied the energies of active helpers. Another activity was the Christian Endeavour Society. Bible classes and sewing classes were also on the agenda. Various people from New Town were Sunday school teachers. Grace, Dolly, and George Wightman, were devoted to their religious work, but also organised various concerts with the children and adults.

Mr. W.H. Teague began his ministry in April 1914, but with the outbreak of war, plus the mission again being in a very poor financial situation, a resolution was passed to close down the mission. This was not taken too kindly by the New Town residents, and they undertook to raise £50 per year to help with the expense. The caretaker and the missionary also agreed to take a reduction in salary, so that the charitable and religious work of the mission could be carried on.

The superintendent of the Sunday school was Mr. Francis Watson Roberts who enlisted for the 1914-1918 war, and was sadly killed in action at Loos on 13th October 1915. At a communion service on February 13th 1916, in memory of their son Francis, Mr. & Mrs. Roberts of South Norwood presented a beautiful carved communion table and four oak chairs. The following year in 1917, individual communion cups were bought for the mission.

Towards the end of 1921 the mission and its missionaries were faced with serious trouble. Mr. Teague became seriously ill and though every attempt was made, it was found impossible to save his life without the sacrifice of his leg. This injury was sustained by a horse kick as a child whilst helping his father in the blacksmith shop. The mission community rallied round, and by their efforts, the mission was still able to function until Mr. Teague was able to resume his duties once more in 1922. Mr. Teague had given service to the mission twice as long as any of his predecessors, but in 1925, he moved on to the Baptist Church in Central Hill. Mr. Martin of St. Andrews, presented Mr. Teague with a silver watch, suitably inscribed for his valued work and assistance. Although the mission now had a new Minister Mr. Teague was still a well known figure with the New Town Community.

In Central Hill, nearby to where Mr. Teague lived, could often be seen standing on the curb, an elderly man with his barrel organ. This was mounted on a two wheel cart, churning out the popular tunes of the day. Perched on his shoulder was a small monkey, dressed in a red coat and hat, looking very cheekily at passers by and rattling a small tin cup. He was a very popular figure with the community. No one knew who he was, although hearsay said that he came from Brixton, but whoever he was, his pitch was always near to Mr. Teague's house and no one ever shouted at him to 'clear away'.

Mr. Teague's vacancy was filled by Mr. Percy Lake of the London City Mission assisted by Mr. Waide who was also the caretaker. Mr. and Mrs. Lake were both devout and tireless workers. In the year 1926, Mr. Lake began a venture which was to become a feature of the district, called 'Happy Holiday Hours'. Meetings were held on the 'rec' for three weeks during the summer holiday season, and they continued for twelve successive years.

The two most important meetings during the week was 'Womans Own', and 'New Town Bright Hour'. Mr. Lake would visit every house distributing New Town news, an evangelical pamphlet. One of the escapades of the boys was climbing onto the roof over the door of the mission entrance, and trying to knock Mr. Lake's trilby off as he came out!!

During 1928 the mission gave a very warm welcome to one of its older members, the Rev. C.E. Rockingham, who gave an inspiring and interesting sermon for the Sunday Service.

Throughout the years the mission had played an important part in the community of New Town. Everyone spoke highly in praise of all the good work that had been carried out and this continued to be, until the final demolition of New Town in 1967.

New Town was situated on the edge of the parish of All Saints which was quite a considerable distance for the people to walk to the Church of England services. In 1895 discussions were taking place with regard to land being purchased in Naseby Road which had previously been the stables of the Victoria Hotel. This building was to be called St. Margaret's Mission Hall, whereby the spiritual guidance of All Saints Church could be carried out and in addition it could provide social facilities for the local community as the following account shows:

An extract taken from the *Norwood News* 1895:

THE ALL SAINTS MISSION NEW TOWN

The important work which has been taken to hand in this locality by Rev. J. Oakley Coles is progressing most satisfactorily, and in no long time will become an active agency for good. The freehold of the site 90ft by 43ft occupied by buildings which were formerly the stables of the Victoria Hotel, having been secured, a contract has been entered into with Messrs I&G Bowyer for structural alterations and repairs, which will cost £242. £200 of this sum has been raised, and, for the balance, donations are earnestly solicited. Many features will be of general un-denominational interest. A gymnasium, a free library and reading room, an infant nursery, a large hall for meetings are deserved of every one's support. The gymnasium will require a special outlay of about £100 and it is hoped that some donor will defray this outlay. The principal building will be adapted as a church, dedicated to St. Margarets and capable of holding a congregation of about 100. The original cost of the site is £800 and to meet this a bazaar is to be held in June.

My Aunt Merce Terry's recollections are that it was really lovely to see the coach and horses arrive for the Sunday services in Naseby Road. The ladies and gentlemen dressed in all their finery, were viewed with delight, as they descended from the coaches.

Central Hill formed part of the boundary between London and Croydon. There were several large residences, and majestic of all was Bloomfield Hall, the residence of Mr. Joseph Tritton. Mr. and Mrs. Tritton organised a great deal of charity work for the neighbourhood. In the early newspapers there are many mentions of beneficiary charities, their grounds opened and teas laid on for the postman, policeman and families, and for many other church outings and functions.

The children now had a choice of two Sunday schools! A good attendance at St. Margarets would mean an enjoyable day at the seaside, generally Bognor Regis, Sussex, or outings held regularly at 'Trittons Fields'. My mother said it was a day they always looked forward to, even though it was only a horse and cart ride from Naseby Road Mission, up Oxford Road, and onto the Bloomfield Estate in Central Hill. The fields were full of buttercups and daisies, and daisy chains were quickly made. After the organised games, each would be given a bun and a glass of lemon, so ending a well remembered day's outing.

Alfred Townsend, uncle to Joseph Townsend has in his possession three books presented to his nephew by St. Margarets Sunday school for good attendance and religious knowledge. There is mention of Joseph later in the book in connection with the first world war. My mother recalled Miss Vyse playing the piano, and many of the older girls helping with the younger children. The service always ended with 'Now the Day is Over' a favourite evening hymn with everyone.

A regular weekly programme would be something similar to this:

Sunday – Sunday School
Monday – Band of Hope

Tuesday – Athletics – vaulting horse etc.
Wednesday – Men's club. Billiards. Chess club run by Mr. Jack Edwards
Thursday – Young ladies 'ping pong' and shuttlecock
Friday – Old tyme dancing & whist drive

St. Margarets also had its own football team, matches played away and on the home recreation ground. The billiard room in the mission was used as their weekly meeting place. My father and Uncle Charlie Terry won medals, with their team winning one of the organised matches.

Mothers' meetings took place in the afternoons, and at a later date the district nurse was in attendance. Earlier in 1896 a well appreciated bath chair had kindly been given for invalids and aged persons.

The boys' club seemed to be a firm favourite with everyone. The curate's wife would read to the boys – hard to imagine a group of boys listening intently to-day! but the reading seemed to be well received. Maybe it was just somewhere to go, especially in the winter months for the warmth and a cup of tea.

Neither were girls left out; the Misses Saunders held a meeting each Thursday evening to teach the young girls of fourteen and over dancing – the cost was 3d per evening. One sister would play the piano and the others would teach the dancing. It was a pleasant evening looked forward to by the girls, and in the break they would receive a cup of tea and a biscuit. Sometimes the girls would give a display of dancing. The boys were envious of them and used to stand outside. Mrs. Baldwin the caretaker's wife would feel sorry for the boys, and let them come into the warmth, providing that they sat still and did not make a noise. When they grew older they were then able to join in with the organised dances held weekly in the hall.

The highlight of the week was the regular 'old tyme' dances where the men met the young ladies and the courting commenced. Many a marriage began at the commencement of dancing cheek to cheek at the mission hall! Mr. Jack Edwards acted as M.C. and ran the dances to raise money for the allotment association. Mr. Carlisle also ran the dances with his wife. Generally there would be a piano and another instrument, and in the interval refreshments would be served.

The mission continued to serve the New Town community in many ways, until finally the building was destroyed by a German bomb in the second world war. Following the elapse of many years the now derelict site was finally sold in 1961. This was a sad ending for a popular mission which had once played such an important roll in the New Town life.

Previously the church services had continued at St. Margaret's mission for four years, until 1899, when land was secured on the estate of the Ecclesiastical Commissioners in Chevening Road, for a new church having a frontage of 150'. The proposed church was a very grand affair, comprising of a church tower and spire, a large central nave with north and south aisle,

St. Margarets Church.

lancet windows, and incorporating an impressive chancel, complete with organ, vestries and chapel, but owing to the high cost, a much plainer church was built. The conveyance of the site for St. Margarets church was on 12th July 1900. Aunt Merce Terry recalls seeing the foundation stone laid on 12th February in 1903 as she ran out of school. In February 1903 an additional 50' was added to the frontage, and later in 1950, a new hall was built on the side, which had been reserved for the completion of St. Margarets Church.

The first minister for St Margarets, 1902-1906, was the Rev. C.C. Gosselin followed by the Rev. H. Lake. The Rev. H. Lake faithfully served his congregation for thirteen years, from 1905-1918. This was one of the very bad periods of unemployment, and the Rev. Lake must have been in despair at the disillusionment that was seen in his parish. I have been told of the many good deeds that he did, and of how kind and helpful he was to his parishioners in this bleak period.

Quite a number of the young boys were in his choir, and for this they would receive a payment of 4/- per quarter, although this was reduced down to 2/- per quarter at a later date.

These are a few names of some of the New Town choir boys, although I am sure there must be many more:

Merce Terry "still going strong" in 1991, aged 101. She is seen regularly at St. Margarets on Sunday mornings.

Stanley Bushel, Sandy Bushel, Albert Land, Leonard Land, Wally Sybald, Fred Beckett, Sid Lewcock, Charles Martin, Frank Martin, Edward Geary, Frank Geary, Sidney Smith James Terry, Joseph Townsend.

The bell of St. Margarets would echo throughout New Town calling the parishioners to the morning and evening service. Mr. Pitt, who lived in Eagle Hill, was the verger and even though he suffered with arthritic hands he rang the bells vigorously. At a later date Mr. Baldwin took over the position of bell ringer. At the time of writing St. Margarets centenary will be near. During this time many people have passed through the doors of St. Margarets. At some time during the course of a lifetime, each and everyone will visit the church, whether for marriage, baptism or death. The church is always there and conveys much more than just an architectural interest, for it embodies the vision and hope of those who contributed, and who were involved with the building as a place for worship for centuries to come.

The church is a haven of peace and tranquillity for all those who need comfort. Week by week, and year by year, whether summer or winter the congregation gathers to sing God's praises and prayers for the world of today and tomorrow.

ST MARGARETS CHURCH

To St Margarets church we used to go,
With many more children that we did know,

Through the gap, as the church bells rang,
Hurrying inside for the hymns we sang.

To stay and watch a baby christened,
At the end of the service, we quietly listened,

Such joy it gave for us all to see,
a baby christened so oftenly.

So this lovely church with its memories held dear,
Continue to serve us year after year,

Built in God's love with mortar and sand,
Its doors ever open for God's helping hand.

MINNIE GEARY

The wedding of one of the Smith family.

CHAPTER THREE

THE NORWOOD COTTAGE HOSPITAL

There had been many mentions of a hospital badly needed in this far corner of Croydon. Patients travelled to Croydon General Hospital for medical attention, then in June 1880, a proposed plan was put forward for public subscription and contributions. Eventually sufficient capital was raised and land was brought in Hermitage Road.

Contributions were acknowledged from all contributors, and subsequently the Norwood Cottage Hospital was built with sufficient room for twelve beds. The first general meeting was held at St. Andrews Congregational Church, Church Road on the 3rd June 1882. The opening ceremony was on the 21st October 1882. A brief description of the hospital is taken from the Sanitary Engineer's report May 1st 1884.

> Exterior of building picturesque, simple but effective, a treatment of English domestic sixteenth-century work. Red tile roofs broken up with gables and dormers, red tile weather tiling and red brick walls. Ground slopes well away from the building. Inside, cheery and bright appearance obtained by well chosen tints and free use of white paint. The walls are warmed by a small iron stoves standing out in the rooms.

The admission of patients except in cases of accident and sudden illness, was by letters of recommendation plus payment for medical attention.

The Norwood Cottage Hospital was very much welcomed, and at one time it was proposed to bring a road through from Oxford Road but this did not materialise. The only entrance was from Central Hill into Hermitage Road, at this time called an 'undeclared public highway', due to it being just a track except for the cobbled stone road leading into the hospital.

The hospital minutes of 1885 mention a wall, and one can only assume that this wall is the boundary wall between the gardens of Oxford Road and the hospital, which can still be seen today.

23rd May 1885

> It was explained that as the proprietor of the ground adjoining had refused to allow any of their land to be used in building the wall it had been found necessary to erect it to one side of the footings instead of in the middle.

At a later date poplar trees lined the boundary between Crystal Terrace and the hospital, and later tennis courts for the nurses were erected on the spare piece of ground in front of the poplar trees. This space is now a car park for the hospital.

NORWOOD COTTAGE HOSPITAL,

PRESIDENTS,

JAMES WATNEY, JUN., ESQ., M.P. | WM. GRANTHAM, ESQ., Q.C., M.P.

VICE-PRESIDENTS.

CAPT. R. WILLIAMSON RAMSAY. | RICHARD THORNTON, ESQ.
JOSEPH TRITTON, ESQ.

𝔓rogramme

OF THE

OPENING CEREMONY,

21st OCTOBER, 1882,

2 p.m. precisely.

STEWARDS.

THE VICE-PRESIDENTS AND MEMBERS OF THE COMMITTEE
OF MANAGEMENT.

In the front door of the hospital was a beautiful stained-glass panel, and nearby a stained-glass window representing the Apostles Peter and John restoring the lame man at the Beautiful Gate of the Temple, together with many other inscriptions of people who had given their love and devotion to the hospital. *(See Appendix 5)*.

In memory of those who gave their lives in the first world war, a plaque was installed by St. Andrews Congregational church, the mother church of New Town mission. A contribution of £1,500 out of the Upper Norwood memorial fund was also given to the hospital in the form of an endowment of beds.

On July 16th 1897, Upper Norwood was gaily decorated with bunting and a triumphal arch adorned with oak and laurel leaves spanning Central Hill. Crowds lined the streets in honour of a visit from H.R.H. Princess Christian of Schleswig-Holstein, who came to receive contributions towards the Diamond Jubilee fund for the hospital.

In the twentieth century a corrugated tin shed was erected at the back of the hospital; problems with tonsils or adenoids were treated in this building. It was very primitive. The doctor just put his fingers down the patient's throat to break them, and then an enamel bowl was thrust under the chin

Norwood Cottage Hospital.

MORTALITY TABLES.

The Compiler and Publishers have been kindly favoured by Edward Westall, Esq., with permission to insert the following tables relating to

THE PARISH OF CROYDON.

QUARTERLY MORTALITY,
January 1st to March 31st, from 1848 to 1855 inclusive.

DISEASES.	1848	1849	1850	1851	1852	1853	1854	1855
Fever	11	13	14	2	5	‡47	6	5
Cholera	0	0	0	0	0	0	1	0
Diarrhœa	5	4	1	1	5	8	3	5
Dysentery	0	1	2	0	0	1	1	0
Scarlatina	4	18	1	0	2	12	5	0
Small Pox	4	3	0	0	0	2	0	0
Measles	24	0	1	0	0	12	3	5
Erysipelas	1	6	0	1	4	8	0	3
Hooping Cough ...	14	4	3	4	3	1	7	3
Disease of Heart...	2	2	4	5	4	10	6	9
,, Lungs ...	68	48	25	38	44	39	43	61
,, Brain ...	6	13	5	13	12	12	19	18
,, Liver ...	1	4	2	4	2	2	2	4
,, Kidney...	2	1	3	3	1	4	2	2
,, Abdomen	18	10	5	8	7	14	6	9
Dropsies	2	1	3	2	2	0	2	3
Convulsions	7	5	7	2	5	9	12	4
*Specific Diseases	0	7	2	2	4	10	3	6
†Other Diseases ...	20	10	11	15	13	22	23	17
Accidents	2	0	0	0	0	1	4	4
	191	150	89	100	113	209	148	158
Per Centage...	0.985	0.762	0.441	0.483	0.533	0.934	0.628	0.618

* Cancer and the like Malignant Diseases. + Old Age, Natural Decay, Debility, Premature Birth, &c. ‡ Typhoid Fever, Endemic.

QUARTERLY MORTALITY at Comparative Ages,
from January 1st to March 31st, from 1848 to 1855 inclusive.

All Ages.	F.	M.	Under 2 yrs	2 to 10	10 to 20	20 to 40	40 to 60	60 to 80	Above 80	Mean Temperature for quarter.	
191	95	96	52	60	11	21	15	24	8	39°.2	1848
150	82	68	33	43	8	21	19	17	9	41 .5	1849
89	46	43	31	9	4	8	18	13	6	38 .7	1850
100	58	42	32	19	5	8	15	16	5	42 .7	1851
113	57	56	37	13	9	12	17	16	9	41 .4	1852
209	102	107	58	39	21	27	28	30	6	38 .1	1853
148	79	69	56	20	6	13	8	34	11	44 .2	1854
158	84	74	42	18	11	21	25	33	8	35 .2	1855

to catch the blood. A blanket was placed around the child, and then mother and child walked home together.

To remove carbuncles, it was a case for a quick cut with the scalpel, used with great skill by the doctor.

Outside the Cottage Hospital encased in one of the stone pillars, was an iron box for voluntary contributions. People who had been treated at the hospital were so appreciative of the care and attention, that they often became regular givers of contributions, no matter how large or small. Mr. B. Poole was one such person following the amputation of his leg.

Each week voluntary contributions and gifts were welcomed by the hospital: flowers, newspapers and magazines, cakes, fruit, new laid eggs, toys, old linen, anything that could be of use would be given. One interesting report at Christmas gives a very good insight as to the care and welfare at the hospital:

> Owing to the fact that there are several serious cases in the wards Christmas this year had to be celebrated very quietly and without song. But what was wanting in this respect was made up for in other ways. By the kindness of friends and sympathisers many useful and welcome gifts were received, enabling the interior of the building to be effectively decorated. Dr. Beaumont thoughtfully gave all the male wards a quantity of 'smokes' whilst the female wards were each presented with a new half crown. Then too, the matron gave all a useful present and co-operated with the staff very heartily in giving everyone under her charge a really jolly time of it. When our representative visited the wards on Friday he found all the patients enthusiastic over the kindness of the matron and nurses.

An incident found in the *Norwood News* – 24th June 1911,

A women named Mary Foote age 71 of Dover Road, New Town, Upper Norwood, slipped on the footpath on Tuesday and broke her leg. Dr. Curling Bates attended and ordered her removal to the Norwood Cottage Hospital.

CHAPTER FOUR

PUBLIC HOUSES

In its infancy New Town possessed only one public house, but this was soon followed by two more.

The first establishment was 'The Eagle', the proprietor Mr. Isaac Smith. This was situated on the corner at the top of Eagle Hill, formerly New Spa Road. Information is very scanty regarding 'The Eagle' but subsequent owners were Mr. William Hayden, Mr. Joshua Radburn and Mr. Henry Dobbs. This particular public house closed at the turn of the century.

Information taken from a local newspaper shows that it had other uses:

1886 January 23rd on Wednesday a meeting on behalf of Mr. Buxton's candidature was held in the large room of 'The Eagle' Norwood New Town.

1886 December 25th New Town Eagle Arms Slate Club. This flourishing society held its annual share out meeting on Tuesday, where the members were much gratified at receiving £1.3s.0d per member. After the share out, a large company enjoyed an evening devoted to music. Mr. Keillen – Treasurer; Mr. Harvey Trustee; Mr. Hughes presided at the piano and sang his favourite song – 'Come into the Garden Maud'. Songs were also given by Messrs. Norris, Wood, Keillen, Land, F. Smith and others. Mr. D. Harvey gave a capital solo on the flute. Usual thanks to the officers and landlord, followed by 'Auld Lang'.

The next public house to open was 'The Oxford Arms' at the corner of Naseby Road formerly Albert Road, the first owner being Mr. William Alfred Abnett. Subsequent owners followed, and the last five in the twentieth century were Mr. Fairclough, Mr. Blackburn, Mr. James W. Bromley, Mr. James Catt Snr., and son Mr. Ronald Catt Jnr. With the re-building of New Town in 1967, the last surviving public house 'The Oxford Arms' was finally demolished, much to the dismay of the inhabitants, as Catt Snr. & Jnr. had been well thought of and held in high esteem by the neighbourhood.

During the intervening years the 'Oxford Arms' had been a popular focal point of New Town. Now in 1967 a new era was approaching without a public house. How the earlier members of the Temperance Societies would have welcomed this event!

The third public house was 'The Fox under the Hill', somewhere halfway down Eagle Hill, formerly New Spa Road and was owned by Mr. Marsh.

Eventually 'The Eagle' and 'The Fox under the Hill' were converted into private houses, leaving the 'Oxford Arms' as the sole remaining public house in New Town. Originally the 'Oxford Arms' belonged to the Huggins

The 'Oxford Arms'.

Brewery, four years later changing to the Charringtons Group, then reverting back once more to J.F. Huggins. It finally changed yet again to Watney, Coombe & Reid. At the time Mr. Ronald Catt took over the business from his father in 1939, Ron and his wife lived above the premises, but at a later date he moved into the house next door and made this his home. The top part was then refurnished to include a games room for the public house.

As in most districts the 'Oxford Arms' was the local meeting point of the working classes. Of its many landlords, one in particular stands out as being a character of note-worthy humour, remembered well by one of the oldest inhabitants, Mr. Horace Margets. Step dancing was popular with most of the men who were encouraged by a barrel organ playing outside. Any girls who were standing nearby would be swung around by Mr. Fairclough the publican, who also possessed a very strong baritone voice, and the residents were quite used to hearing him rendering forth a Victoria ballad 'Let Me Like a Soldier Fall' to the accompaniment of the onlookers who all suddenly appeared.

The 'Oxford Arms' was host to a number of functions – many generations of darts players, the men's club, pub outings and in later years, the loan clubs run by the local inhabitants, a highlight at Christmas being the yearly share-out.

The majority of public houses at this period incorporated a 'jug & bottle' bar. This was a small bar set aside from the main public and saloon bars, where drink could be obtained for consumption off the premises. It was undoubtably one of the smallest of bars, with just room enough to squeeze

Ron and Ivy Catt
at the closing of the
'Oxford Arms'.

in and shielded from view from the other two bars. Hanging up in a long row, was a series of brightly coloured polished copper funnels with long stems, the function of which was to carry the beer when pulled, down to the bottom of the jug or bottle to prevent undue frothing, thus ensuring a full measure of beer.

Adjacent to the counter stood a glass barrel containing large arrowroot biscuits, welcomed by the children while waiting for their parents outside. Previous to 1906, children were allowed to drink beer and enter the public house, but with the new law it was now illegal. The price of beer was 2d a pint or 4d a quart. Money being scarce, the men would have a whip round to make 4d to buy a quart, then share this between them. The well known custom at Christmas was for all the men to receive a packet of cigarettes or a tobacco pouch, and the women were treated to a free glass of their favourite drink. During the year, if tobacco was bought, a free small clay pipe would be given.

Prior to 1914, whisky was 3/6d per bottle. A favourite economical drink with the women was what was called a 'whisky crusher'. This was a small nip of whisky in a glass, to which hot water was added and a lump of sugar. On the counter would be a crusher. This was a glass rod with a flattened knob which would crush the sugar down into the whisky and water, hence the name 'whisky crusher'.

Crown Hill looking towards Crystal Palace, High Level Station and Crystal Palace Tower. New Town is behind the trees on the right of the picture.

CHAPTER FIVE

SCHOOL & RECREATION

The year 1880 saw education made compulsory, the cost paid for by the rates, parents' fees, and a government grant. School was for children aged five to ten years, but by 1900, this was changed making the school leaving age twelve years. In 1918, it was changed again to a school leaving age of fourteen years.

Discussions were taking place regarding a school for Upper Norwood, and eventually Upper Norwood Infants School/Rockmount Primary school was opened on the 21st August 1882.

The total cost of the school building and site was £5684 which caused a great deal of controversy. Correspondence in reports by the school board suggest that the land sold by Mr. E. Bird made no mention that openings from New Town would be walled across. Consequently, after the school was built, 12' walls were erected across two or three openings leading from New Town to the school. This was not greeted too kindly by the residents, as can be seen by the letters between Mr. E. Bird and Mr. Marsh. *(See Appendix 1).* Also a remark by the school board, stated 'what would people think in years to come?'

The following report gives confirmation of the proposed new roads, found in the Health & Sanitary Minutes 1878:

That Mr. E. Bird of Selhurst submits the level of three roads on the Essex Lodge estate Central Hill proposed to be called Rockmount Road, Theban Road, and Troy Road each 40ft wide with sewers and surface water drains shewn to be laid. The application is an important one as it involves the alteration of the course of the Effra Valley Sewer. This sewer crosses this estate at an awkward line for making a road over it and Mr. Bird proposes re-laying it under a new road for which he will ask the board to fix the levels. The new sewer to be 15" instead of 12" as at present and the present application asks for the sewer to be sanctioned from Spa Road (Eagle Hill) to Rockmount Road. The surface water has hitherto flowed down the hollow of the land and a 24" culvert is proposed on the line of the new road as for Rockmount Road.

The committee recommended that the consent of the Board be given to the formation of the three roads in question.

In later correspondence there was jurisdiction over the above, stating that on no account could Theban Road and Troy Road be made into roads, and the 12' high walls were built instead. This isolated New Town from Rockmount Road School. Eventually, an opening was made, direct from

Rockmount School c.1908. In the first row is Charlie Geary and in the second row is George Creasy.

Eagle Hill into the school by a few steps leading into the boy's playground. An alleyway ran along the back of the playground joining Eagle Hill to the main entrance in Rockmount Road, accommodating a well-remembered apple tree.

Whether at this time a wall was also built across the bottom of Eagle Hill is debatable, although there was mention that children were walking out from Oxford Road and down Rockmount Road to the school, which suggests that a wall had been erected. Possibly, with the controversy, a small part of the wall at Eagle Hill was pulled down, thus establishing the well remembered 'Gap' or this could have come later with the establishment of the recreation ground.

In earlier years, Mrs. Dee mentioned that a school was opened in connection with All Saints School, the parents paying 2d per week. Rockmount school catered for all ages; there was a separate infant and junior school. Two entrances led into the building; for the junior school one in the front and for the infants, one in the back. The entrance in the front, led into a small porch, and on the left coats were hung on hooks. All children carried a white hankie or a clean piece of rag, the boys were lucky in having trouser pockets, but the girls would have their hankies pinned to their dresses.

To the right the way led into a small classroom. By the entrance on the left, Mr. Hewlett, the headmaster of the junior school, sat at his desk. Each day a fresh garden flower would be seen in the button hole of his jacket.

The playground at the back of the school contained a tap for water, and by the side hung a metal mug on a piece of string. Also in this playground were the girls offices (lavatories). The entrance into the school from here led up the stairs to three classrooms at the top of the building. Each classroom enjoyed the warmth of a coke fire, and to ensure the safety of the children, large guards were placed around them. A coal scuttle stood nearby.

Miss Povey, the headmistress of the infant school, organised her day in her own room, away from the classrooms. The infants started at four years old and some children at even three years. It was well remembered afterwards how lovely it was to be cosy and warm, curling up in front of the huge coke boiler each afternoon for the rest period.

The infant children would learn by chanting the alphabet, also numbers 1 – 100. Tables were chanted over and over again. All children were called upon from time to time to stand up and read a paragraph. This made them more attentive to the reading that was given.

The main little hall held assembly and morning prayers before school started. There was a first and second bell, and no one dared be late. Sometimes you would get a hundred words to write out if you were late for school. Discipline was a vital part of school life, the children learning obedience and order from a very young age, and woebetide them if they did not keep regular attendance. One stroke of the cane was mainly used for rough behaviour, insolence, direct disobedience, spilling ink, truancy and bad language. Generally it was the boy's escapades that warranted some kind of punishment. More extreme cases warranted two strokes of the cane. Any child who was punished would be entered in the punishment book.

One day my mother blotted her copy book using the standard, nibbed pen and ink, and she was sent to the headmaster for the cane. She explained that it was an accident and that the ink had flowed through too fast. Mr. Hewlett sent her back to her teacher to say that he thought it was an accident, and that she did not deserve the cane!

Mr. Thomas, who took over from Mr. Hewlett, was very strict and would walk round with a hooked cane over his arm. Listening to the mischief of the boys, it was well needed! Because he was Welsh, the children had many lessons in singing, although the school reports seemed to be very favourable regarding the education and learning of the children.

The old proverb of 'Train up a child in the way he should go, and when he is old he will not depart from it' certainly prevailed. Very few children received the cane a second time, the lesson had been learnt. The character building of good decent behaviour is something which we surely could all benefit from in today's world.

Rockmount School c1922. The teachers are Mr. Thomas (left) and Mr. Hedges.
Some of the boys names: Gordon Tripp, Bobby Brown, Bert Simmonds,
Fred Simmonds, Len Wightman, Len Norman, Richard Jones, Richard Horre,
Guy Johnson, S. Pick, Ken Unwin, P. Perkins and R. Palmer.

There were various characters at the school, just as there is today. All the teachers had nicknames. Who ever 'old Grannie Preston' was, I do not know, but she would always give a rap on the back of the knuckles with a ruler, if you were not paying attention. Mr. Batel would creep up behind the children and say "So, you said so and so," then give you a hard flick with his hand.

Various celebrations for special days took place. On the first day of May, known as Maypole day, a post would be erected in the playground, and the children would dance around with long ribbons connected to the post. Empire day, 24th May, celebrated Queen Victoria's birthday, it was officially held for the first time in 1904. The children walked round the school playground waving Union Jacks, and singing patriotic songs.

Once school had ended, the boys made for the rough piece of ground by the side of the school, where the 'gap' was situated. Here also, were two large willow trees which the boys loved to climb. The top of one can be seen in the photograph of Eagle Hill.

In the early twentieth century the girls walked across the recreation ground, and continued down Spa Hill to Ingram Road school for laundry and cookery. History repeated itself again in 1950, when my sisters also made the same walk. Woodwork classes were held at Whitehorse Road School for the boys. It was a long walk in all weathers until finally the classes were changed to Beulah Road School. The seven Terry children all passed through the hands of Mr. Hewlett, so he knew them very well. After he retired, the boys would often wave to him as they made their way home from the Beulah Road class. His house was in Howberry Road, near to the Spa Hill allotments. On one such occasion he gave my uncles a cabbage to take home, a very kind gesture from a very much respected headmaster.

The year 1907 brought changes into the health care of the children, when the school medical service began. Children's hands, nails and hair were inspected. Fleas and nits were a nightmare to everyone, and each evening the mothers would comb through the children's hair, with what was called a 'nit' comb, to see that it was free of lice. If some were found, the hair would then be doused in vinegar, to kill any nits. It did not take long for the unfortunate child to smell like a fish and chip shop!

CROYDON HEALTH – Condition of the heads

Of the 5923 children inspected 130 were infected with live vermin at the time of inspection, and 1334 other children had 'nits' and 89 children had dirty heads apart from vermin. Though the inspection of children in whom vermin were detected at medical inspections remains the same as in 1909 there is a considerable rise in the number in whom 'nits' were found, the proportion having risen from 17 to 25 per cent. This is very unsatisfactory as the presence of 'nits' is a better criterion of the average condition of the children than the number showing vermin, as most children are more or less specially cleansed for medical inspection.

Queueing for the 'nit' nurse.

Rockmount School c. 1930. Some of the pupils were: Doris Smith, Mabel Charlton, Irene Jeffery, Marion Dench, Beryl Tulley, Eileen Dobson, Dorothy Ball, Lillie Farley, Connie Davy.

Rockmount Scool c.1930. A few of the names were: Phylis Jeffery, Barbara Cambridge, Molly Lovejoy, Honour Green, Dorothy Archer, Vera Andrews, Margory Lovejoy, Kathlene Hoad, Doris Hoare, Edith (Tot) Townsend, Daisy Phillips.

The recreation ground which had opened in 1890, was very much welcomed by the school and neighbourhood. The original date should have been May 7th, but due to an unfortunate death, it was postponed, and the grand opening duly took place on May 14th 1890. The cost of the Recreation ground was £9553.

The following is an editorial comment taken from the *Norwood News:*

So far, as we can remember, no such procession has ever passed through Upper Norwood before, as that which assembled in Church Road, and greeted the arrival of the Mayor from Croydon. In all probability it will be many years before such another procession will be seen. The view from the ground in itself is charming. Standing on the brow of the hill, and looking towards the Crystal Palace towers, the red houses dotted about, relieved by the green foliage of the trees, now at their best, offer a charming spectacle.

It is not a bad notion that occasions of this sort should be impressed upon the memory of the children by giving them something to eat and drink. Not only is it useful to do this from an abstract point of view, but good tea with plenty of bread and butter affords actual gratification and pleasure to a large number of poor children, who are allowed to partake.

Then the Upper Norwood Committee very thoughtfully provided gifts of toys which would enhance the pleasure of the day to the children. Displays and demonstrations, carried on throughout the day, together with the local bands. Finally to finish this enjoyable day, a huge firework display shone into the night.

At last the people had something pleasant to think about, and somewhere to go without spending money. There were many comments regarding the cost to the rates, but to the adults and children of New Town, the 'rec' afforded much pleasure, with its bandstand, and open space.

A perimeter fence of posts and iron rails encompassed the recreation ground. The rails were especially enjoyed by the children, whose favourite pastime was using them for turning somersaults. Curved pathways were lined with numerous shrubs and trees, limes, horsechestnuts, plane trees, oaks and many others. Unfortunately, many were felled by the gales of 1988.

Not quite in the middle was the bandstand. No evidence can be found of there being dancing in the earlier years, but definitely in later years the popular night was Wednesday, when people did the one, two, three hop, dancing to the bands that played there regularly.

A tall stone fountain stood nearby, with the inscription:

'Presented by S. Tufnell – Southgate 1891'

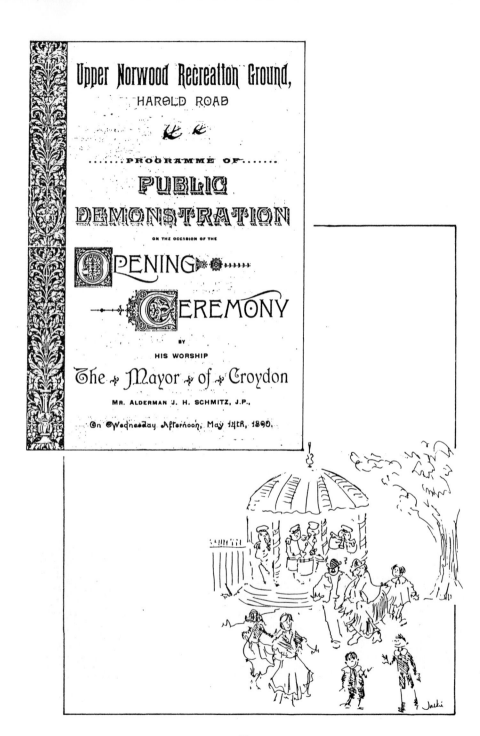

Upper Norwood Recreation Ground,

HAROLD ROAD

........PROGRAMME OF.......

PUBLIC DEMONSTRATION

ON THE OCCASION OF THE

OPENING CEREMONY

BY

HIS WORSHIP

The Mayor of Croydon

MR. ALDERMAN J. H. SCHMITZ, J.P.,

On Wednesday Afternoon, May 14th, 1890.

Adjacent to Eversley Road, a small wooden summer house had been erected with wooden seating inside.

Six iron benches were scattered around the recreation ground, and in the corner a hut for the keeper, Mr. Thomas Moult (called 'old moulty' because he was always complaining about the children of the twentieth century.) Nearby were toilets for Ladies and Gentlemen.

In celebration of the coronation of King George V and Queen Mary, communal school sports were held on the recreation ground, a brief extract taken from *The Norwood News & Crystal Palace Advertiser* June 24th 1911 states:

THE SCHOOL SPORTS

At Rockmount School Upper Norwood, Alderman Joslin representing the Mayor of Croydon briefly addressed about 400 scholars and assisted by Mrs. Joslin handed to them a Coronation medal and bag containing a box of chocolates, cake sweets etc. Headed by Bertram Laud, bearing the Union Jack the scholars marched into the playground where the distribution took place, thence onto the Upper Norwood Recreation Ground, where they were joined by those from All Saints School, Ingram Road and St. Joseph's schools.

Mr. F. Hewlett the head master supervised the scholars' programme, and was assisted by Messrs. Warrington and Garlett (judges) Browne, Buttell

The Recreation Ground showing the bandstand and fountain with St. Margarets Church in the background.

Upper Norwood Recreation Ground showing the bandstand and the drinking fountain.

and the Misses Houghton, Morris and Mason. The infants classes were under the care of Miss N. Burch and Miss Alice Burch.

When the children of the four schools named had assembled at the recreation ground in the spaces allotted to them, they joined in to sing the National Anthem and concluded with three hearty and resounding cheers for the King and Queen. Also present were the Rev. W.B. Taylor Vicar of All Saints Church, and Dr. Curling Bates. The Norwood Town Military Band were in attendance and played selections during the day. Each school contested a number of events for boys and girls, and the successful competitors received prizes from the hands of the judges. Several hundred parents were present and followed the performances of their offspring with apparent enjoyment.

It has always been hard to understand why there were never any swings and roundabouts on the 'rec'. In my time we usually walked to Norwood Park, Central Hill, for this enjoyment. There has always been plenty of space on the 'rec', yet even to-day there is still no playground. But in 1989, nearly one hundred years from the official opening, the recreation ground has four notice boards erected, officially proclaiming its name to one and all!

CHAPTER SIX

NEW TOWN ENCLOSED

The years 1880-1890 saw a change in surnames, but descendants from the earlier generations still remained. Page, Wood, Terry, Hockham, Street, Tyler, Taylor, Harvey, Stevens, Adams, Chamberlain, Dunnicliffe, and many others, whether of the same ancestry or just a coincidence of surnames, is hard to say without verifying. Slowly over the years New Town developed a character unlike any other, and those within its walls developed an identity of their own, which set them apart from the neighbouring inhabitants

Prior to 1895 New Town consisted of three public houses and one mission hall, several small shops, houses, cottages, three roads and two hills encased all around by the varying heights of wall.

There have been conflicting reports as to why the wall was built around New Town. It has been said that it was because of the drunkenness and fighting. Other reports say that it was due to the builders, who were having difficulty in selling their houses built on adjacent land outside New Town. Both accounts seem to be correct. The exchange of letters between Mr. Marsh and Mr. Bird *(see Appendix 1)*, confirm that the builders did have a lot to answer for, but as there was no planning authority at this time, everyone seemed to be able to do as they pleased.

To the west side of New Town, except for the six foot wall between the hospital and the houses, no evidence is available as to why the two high walls were built across the only remaining openings. At this time there was no development on the west side of New Town except for the Norwood Cottage Hospital built in 1882. Disturbances would have upset patients, so perhaps the entrance at the end of Crystal Terrace was blocked by the high wall, keeping any trouble within the bounds of New Town. I have been told that it was a sheer drop on the other side of the wall, so it would have been dangerous for children, especially when the ditch water was running high with flooding.

The period 1880-1890 did seem to be a bad period for fighting and drunkenness. This is confirmed by many of the newspaper reports. Convictions for disorderly conduct, were often given to the same few, although generally, drunkenness was commonplace during this period. New Town did have a bad name, although the archives of the Metropolitan Police have nothing to report on the situation. My researches into the local newspapers have shed no light, except that outside the period mentioned, everywhere was comparatively quiet but during this period too, there were also peaceful times, as the following report shows.

Year 1886 Nov 13th Absence of crime – it is satisfactory to note that no charge has been taken or felony reported at Gipsy Hill Police Station since 29th October.

Year 1887 June 4th Entire absence of crime during holidays – last entry in charge book May 26th.

Nothing has been handed down to me via my family, except that with a few drinks, everyone was merry and bright. You will always get someone who is looking for a fight throughout all history, and I doubt if New Town was any exception. There were many public houses in Westow Hill, and it would be quite easy to imagine a pub crawl with the final fling ending in New Town. Mr. Alan Warwick mentions in *The Phoenix Suburb* that the police stood at the top of Oxford Road in pairs, letting the drunken men in, but would not let them out again.

Where did these drunken men sleep in these five tiny streets, or did they make for the 'gap' and spend their nights on the open ground. What did the ordinary families think of all these disturbances?. I have been told that my grandfather, as soon as he heard a scream, would be out of the door and over the wall like lightning, in case someone needed assistance. In the twentieth century the men knew every brick on the wall, and every foothole. At a later date, the men made step ladders to climb over, as this was still the quickest way by the footpath to Beulah Hill.

Although fighting was commonplace in those days, no one was afraid, for it was always settled by the offended parties. Fights in New Town were always settled at the 'gap', one moment sworn enemies, with 'two bloody noses,' then arms round each other as the best of mates, yet it must have been satisfactory to read in the local newspapers of the day:

> During the Christmas holidays, no police charges have been taken at the Gipsy Hill Station so that all residents in the Upper Norwood district have been on their best behaviour.

A few of the original Woods cottages still remained halfway down Eagle Hill. Adjacent cottages had been added further on, in what was now known by the name of 'Little Eagle Hill' and were still called 'Woods Cottages'. The original cottages were built by Mr. William Wood, but it has not been established whether any of the descendants carried on building. It has been said however, that a Mrs. Wood did own some of the cottages in Eagle Hill, while residing in one of them. The surname of Wood occurred frequently in the area and originally, the fields which surrounded New Town were called 'Billy Woods Fields' and property outside of New Town was owned by a Mr. Wood.

The top part of Eagle Hill was still very steep, with a mixture of houses and cottages. Some had a small garden in the front, while in others, the garden had been cemented over and railings put alongside. The lower part,

'Little' Eagle Hill, consisted of very small cottages, the front door went straight into the house from the pavement. The cottages had two rooms downstairs and two rooms upstairs, with a scullery and lavatory in the back yard. The back yard was very, very small, so the women would string lines for washing from the upstairs windows, across the road, to the large old tree that stood on the other side of the road by the school.

Because the high wall cordoned off the end of Eagle Hill, it was a no through road for vehicles, but the 'gap' in the wall enabled people to walk through. This part was always known as the 'gap' even after the main wall was pulled down. It was sometimes used for some lighter entertainment, especially with wedding celebrations, when everyone would join in.

The Public Health act of 1875, stated that all streets were to be cleaned, paved and lighted, and one can only guess at the number of times the roads may have been cleaned. It was a familiar sight to see the women with a wrap around overall, sweeping the dirt into the curbs, and passing the time of day, intently listening to the latest gossip whilst leaning on their brooms.

Regularly seen was the horse drawn-dust cart. This was like a large box on wheels. Situated on one side was a small ladder with which the dustman climbed up, to tip the rubbish into the box. In some of the houses, the dustmen walked through to the back gardens to collect the bins, and in the summer would sprinkle disinfectant powder into them. The steps of the Naseby Road mission hall saw the men taking a well earned rest, and out would come a can of cold tea and a chunk of bread and cheese for their mid-day break.

Lighting in the area was still very bad. A few dimly lit gas lights were dotted here and there. Mr. 'Wobbly' Watkins, who lived at Queens Road, was the gas lighter man, and tormented by the children who called him 'Walnuts'. He came round every day to light and dampen the street lamps. In Naseby Road, one gas light was in the small alley that ran close to the 'Oxford Arms', the other gas light was by the wall that jutted out at the end of the houses. Mr. Norris generally looked after the gas lights in Naseby Road. The gas light in Crystal Terrace was situated near

Dustmen.

51

to the mission hall, and Mr. Watkins was always annoyed with the children because they had strung a rope around the top to form a make-shift swing. The favourite pastime for the boys was to climb up and swing on the lamp-post rail.

The main thoroughfare in 1900 still continued from the top of Oxford Road. To the right was a piece of open ground, which later saw the erection of the last two houses for New Town, Ayhno & Trefuis, built by Mr. Norris. Running down Oxford Road on the left was a long fence ending at Naseby Road, overhung by a pear tree, which had seen many eager hands trying to touch the pears, or hoping to find some lying on the ground. Many comments were heard to the effect that 'it was en 'ard old pear'!

Two grocers shops, and various houses and cottages, lined Oxford Road, some with side entrances, some with a smallish front garden, trimmed with flowers and hedging. In the early morning caterpillars could be seen weaving their silken webs. The five original houses of Mr. Clapham, called Prospect Place were still standing. Rents were collected by Messrs. Skinners & Co. of Streatham. This association was probably due to one of Mr. Clapham's daughters marrying into the Skinner family.

On the south side of Dover Road, with a shop either end, stood a few cottages of the earlier period. Some were built in pairs, with a small front garden, which were kept very prettily by the occupants. A small pathway led to the front door at the side of the house, and then from there, an entrance led into the long back garden. At the far end of the road were some very bleak looking houses, called Truscott Terrace, not to be confused with the earlier houses that were called by the same name. They had well worn white hearthstone steps, direct from the pavement leading up to the front door. The 12' high wall blocked Dover Road at this end.

The premises on the north side of Dover Road consisted of good-sized terrace houses. They had a small garden in the front, enclosed in the earlier years with iron railings, and a small yard at the back. These yards backed onto the large houses in Naseby Road, which were similar in structure, except that the front door led direct into the passageway from the pavement. A few different houses stood by the 'Oxford Arms', which had side doors, and a few more were erected at the end of Naseby Road. Some became flats, and the remainder cottages, known as Johnny Stevens cottages. Opposite, on the site of the old Eagle Pub, Mr. Fred Keable built two houses.

Two cottages that were my favourites were located at the bottom of Oxford Road on the left, as you came into Crystal Terrace. These were the two original cottages built by Mr. Vinall. They were built horizontally, showing tiny windows in the front, while the rear walls were completely blank. They lay back from the road and had very long front gardens, full of flowers or vegetables, with a hedgerow all around. A wooden trellis was erected around each door, on which grew an abundance of roses, a memory of New Town that I shall always treasure. In earlier years, these cottages had been called 'Vineal Cottages', and the entrance to the mission hall originally led in from these gardens.

The majority of the cottages that had originated at the beginning of New Town all had pretty names, but gradually the names changed, until finally, in 1890, each house was given a number, although even then, the post office always seemed to be re-numbering.

Except for a few small cottages on the North side, backing onto the Cottage Hospital and originally called Comfort Cottages, Crystal Terrace consisted mainly of large tenement houses, said to be the first of their kind to be constructed. At one time there was a plaque above one of the houses showing the date of the first building, either 1851 or 1854. Numbers 1–9, included very large attics. Numbers 11–15 all had an 'airy' in the front, approximately 3'x2' deep, a semi basement area with iron railings as a safety measure. Balls were often lost down the 'airy', and a favourite ball game was often sung:

"One, two, three O'Leary,
My balls gone down the airy,
Don't forget to give it to Mary
Not to Charlie Chaplin"

During the second world war, apart from the 'airys', most cast iron railings were removed for manufacture of munitions to help the war effort. The houses backed onto open land, called Freemans Fields, and they had long thin gardens, which ended with a high wall, each house had casement windows, three in the front, and three at the back. I can remember seeing the curtains pulled back and tied, with an aspidestra adorning the table. Some windows had blinds, and in later years, net curtains were used. As a draught protector, long cloth sausages were made, filled with any pieces of scrap material, and these cloth sausages were put inside the windows to keep the draughts out.

There were several reports of flooding in New Town, and the houses horizontal to Oxford Road were often awash with rain water that would come tumbling down the hill. Mr. Smith's house suffered the most, and the family would quickly lift up two floor boards at the

An 'airy' showing the railings which
protected the drop.

53

Top: Charles Smith with a 1904 Wolseley. Photo taken in 1931.
Above: Mr. and Mrs. James Terry with grandson Bernard.

Top left: Mr. Horace Margets 1990.
Top right: Arthur Land with his grandson John Margets c1929. The 'Oxford Arms' shown on the far left.
Right: Alf Townsend c1925.

boards at the front door, run to the back, and open up the cupboard door under the stairs, to let the rain water run under the house to the cellar, and out into the back garden. Due to this inconvenience, the Highways Department raised the path, so making a deep curb, then split this into two with a step, making it like a double curb. The road itself was very bowed, and a horse and cart had been known to overturn. It was a well recognised fact that a horse would always walk round a manhole ring, never across it.

Located at ground level were well scrubbed white hearthstone steps, which led up to the front door. A hole was drilled halfway down the door to thread string through, and this, when pulled, lifted the latch. A bolt was drawn across at night, but in the daytime, everyone just let themselves in. How trusting people were in this period. The steps led into a passage, where stuffed birds in cases would adorn the walls. Two rooms branched off, and stairs led up to two bedrooms at the top – in one, an iron bed with brass rails and bedknobs, and hidden underneath the faithful 'jerry' pot. A well used marbled washstand, with a bowl and jug stood ready for any new arrivals to the family, plus the ever full chest of drawers.

Direct from the passage, stairs also led down to the basement, where the kitchen and scullery were located. The 'airy' window was in the kitchen, which was always very dark, because it was north facing. The kitchen would have a well scrubbed table and chairs and a black-leaded fire range, with shovel and toasting fork standing nearby. Either side of the fireplace were built-in dressers, where there was an array of china and glass. The floor was either bare, or generally covered with linoleum and home made rugs made out of any scrap pieces of material. A spiral, sticky flypaper would dangle from the ceiling.

In the scullery was a stone floor, sometimes covered with linoleum. Situated in the corner was a cast iron stone boiler, where a fire was lit underneath to heat the water for boiling the washing, This same procedure was carried out for bath nights. Baths were taken in a wooden tub or tin bath that hung on the back door. Friday night was the weekly event for the bath night, each member of the family taking their turn, by following each other into the bath. Hair would be washed first with soda, water and Sunlight soap!

A gas stove was installed, but because it was a penny slot meter and money was scarce, most cooking was still carried out on the kitchen range. A stone sink and wooden draining board completed the picture for the scullery. The basements were very damp, due probably to the river bed that lay behind them. In later years the basements were condemned and everyone was instructed to live on the ground floor, but at the turn of the century everyone still lived in the basement.

1887 saw the invention of gas mantles, but the majority of the houses still kept open gas jets. They gave out a little heat, but with a penny meter, no one used the gas mantles as had been expected. Generally, candles and oil lamps were used, which was more economical. When gas mantles were bought, they invariably crumbled with the slightest touch, which made them useless. How lucky we are to-day, with our world of electrical appliances. How would we survive, if we were taken back to this early New Town without all the luxuries that we enjoy to-day?

Outside was the lav. For seating, wooden slats went from wall to wall, with a hole in the middle. Toilet tissue was newspaper cut up into squares and hung on string. Above the lavatory was the water tank.

Just inside the back door was the coal cellar, and often you would jump with fright if a mouse ran out! The coalman used to carry his sack down the stairs, and through the passageway to the cellar. One cwt of coal cost 1/11d, you could get a bundle of faggots from Mr. Meads the grocer for firewood. A cat was always necessary to keep the mice at bay, and although no one liked the deadly deed, kittens were drowned in a bucket of water as neutering was unheard of, otherwise New Town would have been swarming with stray cats!

Fencing divided most of the houses, and on this grew roses. Most gardens grew vegetables, although some kept bees, rabbits, and chickens. Mr. Fred Smith kept ferrets in cages in his garden, and was the official rat catcher for the Crystal Palace. His brother Ernie who lived next door kept a goat, and was regularly seen with his goat and cart walking home from the Crown Hill allotments, the goat pulling the produce along.

The rent for the Crystal Terrace houses was 5/- per week, and was collected by the rent collector. You were expected to keep the house in good repair and decorative order. If repairs were necessary, such as the roof leaking, you made your own arrangements for the repairs. Because the houses were old, water was always seeping through the roofs when it rained, and the cry of 'buckets' frequently echoed throughout the house.

Bugs were a constant nightmare; it was a regular procedure to inspect the bed clothes every night to eliminate any bugs with a pin. Old furniture was a haven for the bugs, and as furniture was regularly passed around between the tenants, bugs soon spread. It was a disheartening struggle, trying to rid the old houses of these abominable pests. It was generally considered 'a taboo subject', as no one liked it to be known that they had bugs, yet it was universal. According to Queen Victoria's own bug destroyer 'they bit all persons the same'.

Within New Town, people seemed to be on the move all the time, even sometimes back to the same abode! There were probably a host of reasons, yet no one can tell you why. There were always houses to let, very different to today's world! Maybe it was just to be near the grandparents, or for a smaller or larger house, or just the nice neighbours, but whatever the reason, this was the way of New Town life. You could keep moving around all the time if you wanted to. When money was scarce, and the rent could not be paid, you would then move back to a couple of rooms in someone's house, thus making another house empty. Perhaps this was the main reason for so much moving. Outsiders were not very welcome. One tale I heard, was that a family who tried to move from West Norwood, were chased back to where they had come from!

The New Town people were all familiar with each other through long association of previous generations. Men called each other by nicknames or Christian names, but the women and children always referred to people by their surname. No one walked from the house without a greeting being called.

New Town had a variety of nicknames: 'Butty' Rockingham, 'Codger' Gibbs, 'Jim Boy' Terry, 'Grub' Terry, 'Bungay' Biddle, 'Tannet' Biddle, 'Skinny' Biddle, 'Chunky' Charwood,' 'Polar' Wightman, 'Cripes' Geary, 'Tiddler' Terry, 'Goatie' Smith, 'Ikey' Benrose, 'Duccets' Hensley, 'Doggie' Friend, 'Teaser' Bromley, 'Haisy' Hance, 'Ginger' Martin, 'Pickles' Farley, 'Tug' Wilson, 'Topper' Simmonds, 'Topper' Tyler, 'Cokey' Biddle, 'Sacry' Stevens, 'Bogey' Farley, 'Sandy' Bushel, 'Soapy' Taylor, 'Jemo' Bray, 'Red Hot' Tolley, 'Beazer' Burrows, 'Tishy' George, 'Rivers' Cornish, 'Paddy' Uwin, 'Walnut' Watkins, 'Appledasher' Nash, all have a familiar ring to them.

Most villages and towns have a character and lodged in the back yard of Mr. Freeman's, lived 'old Boss'. No one knew who he was, but he helped Mr. Freeman with his barrow and in return was given food and slept in the stables. Everyone felt sorry for him, especially in later years when his health was failing, for all he could do was to stand outside the 'Oxford Arms' selling boot laces. I have tried to find out his name and what finally happened to him, but no one seems to know.

There was also an old tramp called Mr. Terry who wandered in and out of New Town. The Terry name was quite abundant, although not all of the same ancestry. Mrs. Bertha Roberts felt pity for him and eventually after cleaning himself up he went to lodge in her house.

Often being seen pushed along on a large board on wheels, was Sidney Geary. He had become crippled through being badly kicked playing football in his youth. His hobby was making models out of matchsticks. I can remember seeing a lovely model of St. Margarets church with tiny little tombstones. They were all in miniature and must have taken a great deal of patience to construct. As he grew older a three wheeled bicycle was made for him, two large wheels at the back and a small wheel in the front with two handles to help him steer.

In fifty years New Town was now resembling a village community. The boys and girls played together as children, courted each other and in their teens married and bore their children. Everyone seemed related to each other, perhaps this is why everyone seemed so loyal.

The enclosing walls which had once been so opposed, were now a part of the village community. It gave a feeling of companionship, and no one was lonely, grandparents, mothers and children all lived within close proximity of each other. Communal bonds were strong between each neighbour, looking after the children, borrowing a half cup of sugar and other such commodit- ies, especially when the last penny had been used for the gas meter.

The community spirit was such, that if a helping hand was needed, it was always there. The people represented all different levels of working class society; members of the Temperance Society, pub drinkers, regular church members, shopkeepers, publicans and trades- men selling their wares. The regular employed and the unemployed, all living together as a small community in this tiny nine acres of land. It has been said many times to me, that there was no other place like New Town, and from all that I have been finding out, I believe they are right.

Fire! Fire! Fire!

FIRE —On Monday last the South Norwood Brigade were called about 11 p.m. to a fire which was dis- covered in a bed-room in a house occupied by a Mr. Barnes, and partly let out in lodgings, No. 4, Crystal Terrace, New Town, Upper Norwood. The fire was happily extinguished without doing more damage than destroying nearly the whole of the furniture in the room, and causing much alarm to the neighbours. A person lodging in the house is supposed to have maliciously originated the fire; and was given into custody. The furniture was not insured.

The Terry family c1910. Left to right, back row: Elizabeth, Tom, Edie. Granny Elizabeth with Elsie, Minnie, Grandad Thomas William and Tom.

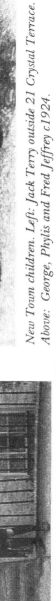

New Town children. Left: Jack Terry outside 21 Crystal Terrace. Above: George, Phylis and Fred Jeffrey c1924.

CHAPTER SEVEN

SHOPS & HOME ENTERPRISES

As the twentieth century dawned, there was still an assortment of shops, and home enterprises, operating in the confines of New Town. The shopkeepers' hours were very long in preparing all the commodities for the shop. Cutting up bacon, cheese, butter, margarine, and slicing cheese with the traditional wire cutter and making up packets of all loose goods.

Food could be bought on credit, and this was called 'penny on the slate'. A small book was kept by the shopkeeper, in which was written all the people's names and purchases, page by page. At the end of the week it would be totalled up, and settlement had to be made, otherwise there would be no credit forthcoming for the following week. Very few people were dishonest, and everything was paid for, even if it meant going without. No one liked a stigma to their name. Morals and pride played an important part in a small community such as New Town. Poverty did not breed undesirables, it only enhanced a conscience of right and wrong. Everyone knew each other too closely, and word would soon get around if someone was in debt. It was a constant and unsuccessful struggle to try and keep respectable, when you were practically living on a 'shoe string' each week.

Not that help was ever refused, as everyone helped each other in what ever way they could. The shopkeepers could barely make a living with all the credit that was owed, yet goodwill and courtesy prevailed. Small talk and inquiring about the health of the family, ensured the custom of the valued customer.

Halfway down Oxford Road stood two grocery shops with cottages between, one of the houses mentioned by Mrs. Dee. This stood back from the pavement, and was owned by Mr. Mead the grocer, whose shop at a later date was brought by Mr. & Mrs. Maxi. The windows were full of different sizes of cardboard boxes full of the commodities that could be bought. At Mr. Mead's you could buy a pennyworth of plum jam, as long as you took your own cup! The cheap jam was called 'Pinks', and was ladled out of a big stone jar. The expensive jam cost 6d per lb. Mustard pickle and red cabbage could be bought similarly, and ladled out into your own dish, and if you took your own bottle, a pennyworth of vinegar could be obtained. On the ceiling of the shop, hob nailed boots were strung up. A scheme had been devised at Rockmount School for the children to take a halfpenny or penny, and this would be entered onto a card. As soon as enough had been saved, a ticket would be given, enabling the mothers to buy clothes or useful items both at Mr. Mead's shop and at Uncles, another shop similar to Mr. Meads. These were the only shops where the tickets could be changed.

Two cottages along from Mr. Mead's shop was Mr. Gwyers. This shop mostly sold confectionery and biscuits, both whole and broken biscuits. When Mr. Bromley (Teazer) and his wife Maria eventually took the shop over they changed to selling greengrocery.

In the corner of Dover Road and Naseby Road opposite the corner of Eagle Hill, stood the baker's, owned by Mr. Townsend. Between Mr. Hance, the bootmaker, and the baker's, stood a large tall chimney for the bakery. It was a real delight to smell the home baked bread. which did not take long to sell, as this was the only bakers in New Town, and made enough bread to sell each day. Consequently, there were no stale cakes or bread that could be obtained cheaply.

The baker's was sold at a later date, and bought by Mr. Plumridge who ran the premises as a newsagents and confectioners. There was a grand variety of toffees all sold at 4ozs a penny.

Diagonally across to the opposite corner stood Mr. Tietgens, a grocers shop. Here you could buy half the top of a cottage loaf for one penny, or the bottom half being larger, for twopence. This shop ran a Christmas club where you could put a farthing or halfpenny on the card, and this would bring in extra goodies for the Christmas festivities.

In Oxford Road on the corner of Dover Road Mr. & Mrs. Tyler ran the greengrocery store. They lived at the bottom of Eagle Hill, but after their daughter married Mr. Wilson, they gave up the shop to their daughter and son-in-law. Mrs. Wilson was a great friend of my grandmother Annie Geary. The horse and cart was kept in the stable behind the shop, and beetroots could be seen being boiled, with the horse standing nearby.

The shop that the children liked best was Polly Brand's sweet shop, which was located at the bottom of 'big' Eagle Hill. The shop always seemed to smell of pickled onions! Eagle Hill was divided into two parts, where the break came in the middle. The top part was soon nicknamed 'Big Eagle' and the lower part – 'Little Eagle' When you walked into Polly Brand's shop, a large bell which hung on a spring over the door, rang out. There were all kinds of sweets, port wine toffees, tiger nuts, and lace licorice, – many different from those we know today. You could buy a 'happorth' or 'pennorth' of sweets, or a single liquorice for a 'fadger' (farthing).

Jack's shop (Mrs. Wilson) stood at the bottom of 'Little' Eagle. Here you could buy cigarettes, newspapers, and sweets – hot drinks could be obtained from the back of the shop. All the children liked the lucky dips, and for 1d you could choose an envelope in which was written the lucky gift obtained from the counter. This shop stood by the side of the 'gap'.

A few cottages along, Mrs. George used the front room for selling toffee apples and sweets.

There were three boot repairers, or 'cobblers': and with all the walking that everyone did, surely this was the best trade to have.

General shop.

Mr. Styles	Bootmaker	Lived next door to Mr. Bromley's shop, Dover Road.
Mr. Hance	"	Lived at the corner of Naseby Road.
Mr. Harvey	"	Lived at the beginning of Dover Road, opposite Mr. Tyler's greengrocery shop.

In today's society, where money is easily obtained by credit cards, the pawn shops have virtually ceased to exist. They were commonly called 'Uncles', and outside would hang three balls depicting the kind of shop that it was. To those people who found themselves in difficult circumstances, this was the only way that credit could be obtained. The extra money would help tide you over until next pay day, or when the financial situation improved.

The two nearest pawnshops to New Town, were Messr. Rutters, Gipsy Hill, opposite Cawnpore Street, and Messrs. Bryce & Son, High Street, West Norwood. One interesting tale regarding the pawn shop related to a Mr. Jones. One day he was offered a painting job by Mr. Keable, the builder. At this time workmen supplied their own tools for the job, but unfortunately Mr. Jones had previously pawned his distemper brush and now much to his embarrassment sadly explained why he could not take the job. Luckily, Mr. Keeble lent Mr. Jones the money to retrieve the brush from the pawn shop, and all was well.

Almost any household item of value could be taken to 'Uncles'; the family heirloom, the Sunday best suit, jewellry, vases, shoes, anything that would bring in a few coppers. It would be taken in on a Monday and redeemed on Friday ready for the weekend. New sheets and items such as those bought from the tally man on tick would never see the light of day. They would stay in the original wrapping paper, being used as collateral week after week. All these items would be neatly wrapped into a paper parcel, securely tied, to await redemption on the next pay day.

At the pawn brokers, interest was charged at a halfpenny for every 2/- loaned for a period not exceeding a calendar month. It would be extra money if time elapsed over the month. On the ticket would be clearly printed the conditions of the transaction. In 1872, an act was passed to consolidate all acts relating to pawnbrokers in Great Britain. Any goods pledged and not redeemed could be sold after twelve months and seven days from the pledge. At the end of that time pledges pawned for 10/- or under became the property of the pawnbroker. Pledges over 10/- had to be disposed of by public auction. Subsequent to the above, there were alterations to the act in 1922 and 1927.

The 'Tally' man came cycling into New Town each week hoping to make new transactions, plus collecting the weekly amounts and hopefully something off the arrears. As soon as he was seen many individuals hid to create the impression that no-one was in the house. Vouchers in lieu of payment would be given and these could be used for clothes, bedding etc., obtained from their local agents. Messrs. Bryce in West Norwood dealt in this kind of transaction. It was popularly called the 'never, never', as with the interest you paid, you 'never' did get clear of the debt. If the tally man's bike was seen outside a particular house for a prolonged period, it soon led to idle talk and speculation by the gossips. Was he collecting more than just a few coppers?

Several of the New Town people kept two wheeled hand carts for selling their wares. These they would push up to Westow Hill. Westow Hill at this time would be lined with coster barrows between the 'Holly Bush' Public House and the 'Albert' Public House. Mr. Farley often had 'one over the eight' as he wheeled his barrow home from Westow Hill into New Town. He could regularly be heard singing all the old songs as he made his way home. Singing by everyone seemed to be quite a regular occurrence after they had had a few drinks, and no one thought anything of it, as it was all quite harmless, and often provided some entertainment.

Various people used their parlours or front rooms to make extra cash. Laundry was the most popular. One house would labour at the washing, another the mangling and yet another the ironing. As can be seen from Victorian photographs, clothes for the body were numerous. Young ladies wore a combination, chemise and fancy bodice, flanelette and embroidered petticoats, a loose smock dress, and the young girls a pinafore, with wide and narrow ribbon threaded through. A great deal of washing was needed when the family was large, and consequently laundry work was given to a great number of the labouring poor.

Mrs. Archer was quite a character, who lived at the end of Crystal Terrace by the side of the high wall. As soon as she heard any children near the wall, she would run up the steps and shout at the children to 'get off that wall', perhaps not always in the best of languages!! She did the washing and ironing for the gentry year after year, and it would be collected and returned in a basket on wheels. She was often seen tottering down from the 'Oxford Arms', after having 'one too many'. In the later years, when she was really old, she would pay the children a few pennies to take the basket backwards and forwards to Beulah Hill for her. There was always a smell of washing as soon as the front door opened, as she must have been doing this kind of work for over forty years.

Halfway down 'big' Eagle Hill, stood Mrs. Sibbald's house, which was always very dark inside. She was a firm favourite with the children, selling sticky toffee apples! In the yard at the back of the house, a sack of coal could be obtained. Mrs. Sibbald was also the recognised money lender of New Town, charging 25% interest on transactions.

Also in Eagle Hill, Mr & Mrs. Gibbs grew flowers in their garden, and sold them to the public. They could be seen in a vase standing in the window or sometimes in containers by the gate. Many bought the flowers for remembrance, on visits to Queens Road or Elmers End Cemeteries.

All the houses had open grates and coal fires. Mr. Gibbs was the local sweep known locally as 'Sweepy', and he was a well known figure carrying his brushes upon his shoulder as he made his way to sweep the chimneys. The brushes were kept in a shed in Oxford Road, although his house was located in Crystal Terrace,

Some people would try and sweep their own chimney, and Mr. Guy Johnson thought he would try to do just that. He borrowed a sweep's brush from Mrs. Smith, climbed on top of the roof, looked around, but then did not know which was his chimney top! To find out, he threw a few bricks down the chimney, hoping to hear his wife shout, instead of which, it was another neighbour shrieking that things were falling down her chimney and the parlour was covered with soot! To add insult to injury, when he finally started to sweep his own chimney the brush got caught and he ended up burning it out!! So instead of saving money it ended up a costly business, with him buying a new sweep's brush for Mrs. Smith.

CHAPTER EIGHT

STREET CRIERS

Various tradesman found their way into New Town, selling their wares from a horse and cart. The fishmonger's familiar cry was:

"Come out wiv yer dishes, I'll fill it wiv little fishes."

This tradesman sold mostly loose sprats, and the basins were soon overflowing.

Mr. Dove, whose shop was in the High Street, West Norwood, drove in with his pony and trap selling cat's meat. It was sold on a long wooden skewer. If there was no one in he would leave it under the knocker of the house. They were large ornamental cast iron knockers, size about 3"x8". All the cats knew who he was and would follow him around New Town.

There was also a vendor who sold concentrated carbolic solution, which was the main cleaning agent. The householder took a bottle out to him and he would fill it up for one penny. The carbolic was badly needed for the old toilets, sinks and water tanks.

Another travelling tradesman would mend pots and pans with his soldering iron while you waited and passed the time of day with him or viewed the windows to see whose curtains needed washing!! The salt man with his large block of salt would cut it to the size you required. This was generally a job for the children, who then cut the salt into small cubes to fit into a jar ready for use with cooking.

The oil man sold paraffin, white hearthstone for the steps, and Zebra blacking for the fire grates. The scissor grinder came pushing his small cart with the grinding wheel raised on top. He would knock on the doors, asking if there were any tools that needed sharpening and people would wait and chat while they were sharpened.

The rag and bone man with his horse and cart was a very familiar figure. His bell rang vigorously to accompany his familiar cry of

"Any old lum — ber, rags, bottles, or bones?"

He would take practically anything. A few old rags wrapped up like a ball would fetch a copper (penny), or sometimes he would pay with a goldfish in a bowl, much to the delight of the children.

Sea fish food was always welcome as it was the traditional cockney tea for Sundays. Mr. Farley's cry would ring out
"Winkles, they're lovely."

and Mrs. Tyler would come round with her basket of shrimps during weekdays.

Along would come the muffin man, ringing his bell and balancing a tray of muffins upon his head. The well known nursery rhyme reminds us of his popularity, and was sung many miles from Drury Lane;

'Have you seen the muffin man,
the muffin man, the muffin man,
Have you seen the muffin man,
who lived in Drury Lane

The haberdashery man sold all kinds of coloured cottons, ribbons, elastic, tape, everything for the mother's workbox from his tray. His favourite call was:

'Four yards of tape – a – pen-ny.'

The flypaper man was a comical sight. He wore a high top hat, around the middle of which he had wrapped a length of fly paper. He always called out in a very strong voice:

'All the tormenting flies, catch them alive.'

Mr & Mrs. Freeman who lived next door to the school, sold rabbits and fish. Their daughter Lizzie came round the houses carrying a large wicker basket filled with fish.

Anything that was bought in a container would have a refund on its return. One chappie would come round blowing a bugle, to let you know that he was in the street. He encouraged the children to bring out any bottles or jars to him, and for these he would give a paper windmill. You can imagine the bargaining that went on between mother and child, the child wanting a windmill, yet the mother knowing that she would get a farthing or halfpenny when it was taken back to the shop.

Sundays saw 'Jim Boy' carrying the beer around in open quart cans. At the public house you could buy a quart of beer, but because of the spilling, the quart cans were only filled to a pint and a half. They were carried on a long broom handle with hooks fixed into it, and these hooks held the cans. For those that were aged and lived at the bottom of Eagle Hill, 'Jim Boy' must have been very popular, as the hills were very steep when you were finding it hard to get your breath. Again it was a penny on the can for its return.

One of my grandfathers lived at 26 Oxford Road. This had a very large garden which ran down to the back of the hospital. Bee keeping was his interest, and he edited and printed a Bee Keeping journal for two years. Mr. Smith the greengrocer kept his horse and cart in the garden and other people kept their horses in there also. The garden had an extra entrance which led in from an alley in Crystal Terrace. It was another enterprising venture as apparently he used to charge for horses, carts, and bikes etc. to be kept there.

Mr. Smith never changed his 'calling' throughout all seasons, as he sold his greengrocery around the streets:

'Luv-er-ly ripe straw-ber-ries.'

Sunday was the day for the Italian ice cream man. Most of the ice cream

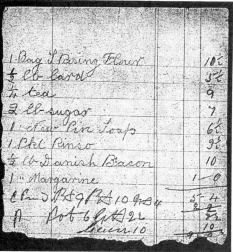

A shopping list c1925.

Some of the street traders.
Right: the muffin man.
Below left, a knife grinder
and right, the barrel organ.

The milk delivery cart.

was made by the Italians in the early years. When errands by the children had been run, an 'appeny was often given and this would be saved for their favourite ice cream. The ice cream cart was pulled by a donkey, it was a father and son business and the ice cream was sold loose. The children soon found out that you got more in a glass for a penny, than you did in a cup!

Milk could be brought from the shops in a jug although a milkman did come round with a cart that he pushed himself. One pint of milk cost 2d. The skimmed milk was kept in large churns and he would ladle it out into a jug, the charge being 1d a pint. Mostly, the poorer families used condensed milk as this was much cheaper and lasted longer. There were no refrigerators and the only way to keep things cool was in a bucket of cold water with a damp cloth over the top.

Cows were regularly seen being driven to what was called the top fields. Bells hung round their necks and an old lady would keep calling to them to 'move on'. They came from Frenchie's dairy in Cawnpore Street and were driven up Lunham Road, through Harold Road and into the fields. The manure from the horses and cows was invariably quickly shovelled up to put on the allotments and gardens. In fact two enterprising young lads, the Bray boys, did collect the manure and charged one penny per bucket.

The horse and cow manure attracted plenty of flies. Everything indoors was covered with little net covers on which beads were sewn along the bottom, this added extra weight to enable the covers to stay on.

CHAPTER NINE

POVERTY

Unemployment and poverty go hand in hand, yet listening to this younger generation complaining about their plight, one wonders how they would fare if the clocks were turned back and they were shown just how terrible poverty really could be. By the turn of the century things were really bad and continued to be so. Unemployment had been steadily getting worse since 1880 and persisted until the general strike of 1926 and even beyond. There were no social services, no unemployment money, and if your husband died, no pension. If the parents died, the children survived the best way they could.

In the nineteenth century and indeed even before, as far as the rich were concerned poverty was the consequence of idleness or lack of thrift or drunkenness and any other vice you care to mention, but by the early twentieth century attitudes were changing. It was now realised that poverty might not be the fault of the poor but could be the result of misfortune, or circumstances over which the worker had no control.

England's labour force was subject to much suffering in this bleak period. Had the labourer not been attracted to Norwood by the prospect of employment at the Crystal Palace, unemployment would have been encountered elsewhere.

How did the working class families survive? It is hard to imagine that every crumb and every farthing counted. Organised unemployment marches were seen regularly singing around the streets of Norwood. The start of the singing was:

Help the unemployed, We're starving day by day,

with the men rattling tins for a collection. Dr. Sharman and the Rev. Walter Hobbs organised many of the marches, as this account from the *Norwood News* shows:

February 23rd 1895 – THE UNEMPLOYED

During the continued frost, efforts have been made in the district to assist the poor both by private help and by the committee for the unemployed men. The working men had a march out on Monday, assembling at 7.30am starting at eight o'clock. About 230 were in the procession, the sum of £33.5.10d being collected by the men in the boxes they carried. The treasurer (Dr. Sharman) received £67. Married men received 7s.6d and single ones 6s. This followed a payment of the previous week and one on Wednesday last. There will be another payment to the men to-day

(Saturday). The Rev. Walter Hobbs marched at the head of the procession on Monday for more than four hours. The free bread and milk breakfasts at Gipsy Road Baptist Chapel have been largely attended at each meal. The soup kitchen at Emmanuel Hall has been in full swing.

Sometimes there would be work at the Croydon council yard called Appleyards. Men would sit on a large stone or box and break stones with a hammer, these were used for the building of roads. It was called "2½ macadam". You were paid 2/6p for a hard day's grind. Many a back was aching after bending double nearly all day. When my uncle first told me this, I did not realise that 'macadam' was actually named after John Loudon Macadam, 1756-1836. He is responsible for our good roads, and even to-day, roads are 'Macadamised' The method was to put large stones down first, then fill in with smaller stones, and finish with powder ground from the stones themselves to fill in the gaps.

During the winter months a fall of snow would be a blessing, whereby a few pennies could be gained by sweeping snow all day – a back-aching job. Many suffered afterwards with coughs and colds due to the flimsy clothes that they wore. For those labourers who were skilled at plucking poultry, jobs were available before the Christmas period. This extra money helped to tide the families over the leaner days. Often giblets were boiled up into broth and handed around to those less fortunate.

Central Hill, Church Road, and later Harold Road, all consisted of very large houses, employing many servants which gave work to the poorer classes. The women sometimes had several jobs and walked miles from one to another, generally working as a charlady or if they had been in service, then sometimes as daily maids. It was the only way to keep their large families in food and clothing. Often they would get the cast off clothes, or the remains of food to take home to their hungry brood. The children always looked forward to their mother coming home as they knew she would often have cold toast or 'scraps' for them.

The owner of one house at the top of Sylvan Hill who employed my grandmother, let her bring all the coal dust home in her apron. As soon as she was near the house, she would call to the children to bring out a bucket to tip the coal dust in. What endurance this generation had! She must have lived by the motto 'Waste not, want not'.

Washing and ironing for the employer was sometimes carried out in the home. Hard to imagine in today's world the hard work involved, yet everyone took pride in a line of white washing blowing in the breeze. First they would bring in the dolly wash tub and add a handful of soda crystals to the water. The clothes were then put into soak, using a dolly stick to help free the dirt. A fire was lit under the 'copper', this was a cast iron boiler cemented close to the wall. The lid was wooden which fitted tightly over the opening at the top. After soaking, the clothes were then scrubbed with a stiff

REVIEWS AND REFLECTIONS.

The severe visitation of frost, which has been so trying and has left so much distress amongst the poor, has effected one social benefit which will to a great extent compensate for its hardships. Water has ceased to flow and the earth has been as iron, but men's hearts have been melted into tenderness, and the streams of charity have issued from their sources with a volume which resembles the rising of the Nile, and promises to fertilize anew the frozen fields of industry. Like other visitations, the frost has been a blessing in disguise. It has created suffering and it has generated sympathy; it has arrested labour and it has liberated love; it has inflicted privation, but it has taught generosity. The social nightmare of "masses and classes" has vanished; the sufferings of the poor have been a sorrow to the rich; the willingness to help has been equal to the want of help; and inability to give more has probably been as keen a trial as the need of more. We know ourselves better now than we did a month ago. We have found out, what we too easily forget, that we are all of one family: poverty and wealth are less suspicious of each other, and brotherly kindness is growing apace. This is a salutary change, and will outlast political panaceas. It is true in all directions, and not least in this neighbourhood. There has been everywhere a spontaneous outburst of liberality. In Croydon £700 had been subscribed a week ago; this week will probably make it £1,200. In Upper Norwood the vicar of All Saints' received £50 for an Emergency Fund in a few days. Acknowledgment is also made in a letter from Rev. J. G. Train and Mr. Allan Keiller of considerable contributions to an Unemployed Working-men's Relief Fund. The Parish of St. Luke's, Woodside, is emulous of a like distinction, and earnestly solicits assistance for many who are in urgent need. West Norwood has been well looked after by Rev. Walter Hobbs, as reported under local news. South Norwood has exerted itself in the same direction, with very creditable results. For more than seven years it has possessed an excellent society under the admirable name of the Samaritan Society. The benevolent scope which that implies is at once recognisable, but it stands for something more. It means undenominational co-operation. It appeals to all for help, and it withholds help from none who are deserving and in any kind of need. The enlargement of this society's benevolence during the present distress has been undertaken by an enlarged committee, and its appeal for special support has already resulted in donations to the extent of £100. This is very gratifying, though it may not be sufficient. Gifts must be multiplied, and there is also a demand for loans. The honourable spirit of independence has induced some to say that they would like to repay any sum that may be advanced to them, and the committee have consented to make such advances. They have also decided to give free breakfasts of bread and milk to 100 poor children, and free dinners to the most needy and deserving. There is, therefore, need of a prompt reply from all who have not yet given, and if the many will give their little, and the few their much, the next few weeks will enrich South Norwood with a nobler reputation than it bears even now.

Men waiting for work.

Washing day.

brush on a wooden scrubbing board using Sunlight soap to clear away the
heavy grime.

Once the water had boiled in the copper, soap powder was added plus
all the white clothes. After boiling, the clothes were lifted out with the
wooden copper stick (often used to threaten the husband and children) and
then rinsed several times. Finally, for the last rinse, a Ricketts blue bag was
added, this was like a small blue muslin bag and the blue would be swished
round in the rinsing water to help make the clothes whiter. Men's shirts and
collars were all starched and starch was made up from a packet of powder
which dissolved in boiling water. Outside was a large iron mangle with a
handle to turn the large wooden rollers, these would then press out all the
surplus water.

Ironing for the weekly wash was never ending; first iron blocks were
heated on an open fire, these were then inserted into the interior of the iron
through a little trap door at the back. A later innovation saw the arrival of
the flat iron which dispensed with the iron blocks, and with the advent of
gas, ironing was made easier by heating the irons on the gas rings.

They were long hard days, and the domestic work for the women would
be from about 8am to 6pm. Grandparents mostly looked after the children

which was their way of helping to pay for their board and lodging. The elder children also took their turn in caring for their younger brothers and sisters.

Statistics show that one in five houses employed servants towards the end of the 19th century. Over a million women and girls were in private service. Sometimes the girls would be so small that they could hardly reach the sink. It was taken for granted that domestic servants were a fact of Victorian life. Most girls would be in service until they married, then with the knowledge that they had acquired they were able to resume their duties with their employers on a casual basis.

As has been stated, New Town did have a very bad name, and when my mother first applied for her household job, Dr. Eccles straight away said, 'No good ever came out of New Town'. But Mrs. Eccles was very adamant, and said that my mother had a very good reference from the Rev. Lake and that her family were honest and hard working, she felt it only fair to give the girl a try. In fact when my mother was taken away with diphtheria, her employers were very kind to her and sent food and books to the hospital.

Searching through archive records, I realise now why this was said, as her employer, Dr. Eccles, was a well known figure in the Temperance Societies, and with most of the meetings held in the mission hall in New Town, he knew just how bad the drinking problems were there.

There was a great deal of charity work carried out for the poorer people, soup kitchens were being mentioned as early as 1887:

1887 February 5th The bread and milk breakfasts for children at Gipsy Road Chapel continue to be well patronised, one morning about 400 children attended. We hear of some little girls who went to a soup kitchen with dinner tickets and found there were no dinners left. This perhaps is unavoidable, but it causes a great disappointment.

These terrible conditions continued for the unemployed well into the twentieth century.

Food was always rationed out within the families. Generally the children's day started (if it wasn't their turn for the early morning shopping), by the eldest being given a slice and a half of toast and dripping. This was toasted on a long toasting fork in front of the coal fire. The next eldest was given a slice, and the younger children half a slice each.

As soon as the children were old enough, they would take their turn in the food scramble! In the early hours of the morning they would go running out of New Town, trying to be first in line at the baker's shop, hoping for any stale bread or buns left over from the previous day. A candle would be lit and the mothers would tell them to be careful as they raced around to try and be first in the queue, after gulping down a mug of cocoa to try and help keep out the cold. The first baker's was at the top of Harold Road. Often Mrs. Lee would come out and tell them not to make a noise as it was just six o'clock in the morning! It was a long time for the children to wait, and one of my

London children at a soup kitchen.

aunts actually fainted with hunger whilst waiting for the door to open.

Eventually the shop door would open and the children held out their pillow cases and said "Have you a 'pennorth' of stale bread, please", and Mrs. Lee might say, "Only enough for three", but by the time the sentence had finished the children were off and up to the next bakers. Sometimes they ran as far as the bottom of Anerley Hill or Gipsy Road hoping for something to take home. Often they were disappointed and their mother would say "Oh well, we will just have to make do".

This running around was all before school time and by the time they got to school, the second bell had rung and then they were reprimanded for being late!

A meeting on the plight of the children was reported as:

CROYDON'S STARVING CHILDREN

The demonstration on Sunday at Croydon in favour of Croydon feeding its starving children out of municipal funds and not voluntary effort, was a fiasco as far as numbers were concerned. However, this did not interfere with the spirited character of the speeches.

Mr. H.T. Muggeridge, who presided, in the course of his remarks said Croydon was, in proportion to its size, a very wealthy town, but at the same time there existed a great deal of poverty, and the question of feeding the hungry children was urgent. The school canteen Committee had the chief control of it, and in their report they expressed great satisfaction at the assistance given by teachers etc., in investigating cases, and in undertaking part of the work in distributing dinners. But it was not a very generous committee, for no child received both a breakfast and a dinner. A lady speaker Miss. McMillan, argued that before a child could receive instruction, it must be physically fit. Many children were not in the least fit to receive to instruction which was held out to them.

Their idea was to make all – rich and poor – unite in the cause of the children to see that they were sufficiently and properly fed, and also to see that under the present conditions, their education system was but a "Nervous System". This was not Socialistic it was humanity. Mr. George Lansbury, speaking, not as an expert, but as an ordinary man looking around the schools said he found in the East End of London and Croydon too, it was only too evident that the majority of parents could not afford the necessary money for providing children with clothing and food. With regard to parental responsibility, he thought that was broken down by elementary education itself; if the child required food there was the duty of the state – to supply the food. Mr. G. Young proposed a resolution in favour of putting in force the Underfed Children's Act and this was unanimously agreed to.

Other meetings and newspaper articles eventually led to Croydon opening the 'Mayor's Fund for Underfed School Children'. One article mentioned:

Of what good were reading or arithmetic; who could learn laundry or cooking when listless and apathetic from a continuous diet of bread and milkless tea, so inevitable when the wage-earner is without work for months at a time.

But until the wheels were put into motion, people carried on foraging for food and tried to feed their children on the meagre portions that were available.

The Poor Law had changed very little in the intervening years since the days when my grandmother was a little girl, life was just a continuous struggle, but in 1905 James Ramsey McDonald, one of the labour statesmen, empowered local authorities to establish distress committees to assist in finding work for the unemployed, relief aided by a government grant.

By 1906 meal tickets could be obtained from school due to the Education Committee Act, and if you went regularly to Sunday school you would also get a meal ticket and be able to go to one of the organised soup kitchens that had been set up. One of these places was in Gipsy Hill next to the police station. The child would run all the way during the school lunch break and then be given a cup of haricot beans, potatoes, some kind of meaty gravy, a crust of bread and a mug of water. Then running all the way back again he or she would be just in time to hear the second school bell ringing.

The first one home from school would take an enamel jug and run down to Beardell Street, just off Gipsy Road. Tickets were exchanged for a ladle of greasy soup with a crust of bread. It was only old bones boiled up and to the children it looked like dirty washing up water, but everyone was glad to eat anything to ease the gnawing of hunger pains.

Occasionally tickets would be given out at school for provisions from the Salvation Army. One day everyone queued up for frozen fish and each was given one fish, someone at the back called out, 'Tell him to leave the eyes in, so it will see us through to the end of the week'! Sometimes someone would hear of free soup being given away and everyone would run to the said place only to be disappointed when they found out it was only a rumour.

These extra provisions to help the families must have been a real relief to the mothers and eased the constant worry of how to feed their large families.

The children would also go on a shopping expedition to Westow Hill. First to the butchers to get what was called a 'sixpennyworth of fry'; this would consist of maybe a sausage, bits of liver, or an odd chop, all wrapped up in a piece of newspaper. On return home it would all be sorted out so each of them would get something at mealtime. The best value was when it was meat for a stew, as you could make it last for several days. Food was a constant worry when you had seven or more mouths to feed. Popular meals were toad in the hole; meat pudding; bacon pudding; shepherds pie, and bread pudding eaten cold as well as hot.

Sometimes you could buy three 'pennorth' of pork rind and bones to make brawn jelly, or three 'pennorth' of cracked eggs, always broken in a cup first, as many of the eggs would be bad. A pennyworth of wet fish was similar: either a kipper, cod or mackerel. Also vegetables, were asked for as a 'pennyworth of potherbs, please'. This was made up from carrots, turnips, parsnips, anything that was a bit substandard. Cheap fruit could be bought as a 'pennorth of specs'.

At weekends, half a pig's head or sheep's head would be bought, and this could be turned into a stew for the next couple of days providing that there were plenty of vegetables to add to it. An old black saucepan always stood on the side of the fire for any scraps of food, everything was put in to make a good stock.

On some occasions casual work would be available on Saturday and with the extra money, a flank of beef or breast of lamb could be brought on Sunday mornings from the butchers in the High Street, West Norwood. The smell of roast meat wafting through the streets of New Town gave the more fortunate of the community a feeling that it was still a traditional Sunday.

Can we today really imagine the fear of being thrown out onto the street? But this did happen. Each family knew that the main aim was to keep a roof over their heads, for in this way they could still get by, even though the 'tummy' might feel empty. The first priority was to see that the rent was paid, then what was left was spent on food. If someone along the road was unable to pay their rent, then a collection would be made until a sufficient amount was collected. The rent was always kept in a jug upon the kitchen mantelpiece, and everyone was brought up to be thrifty and honest.

During the winter months, extra blankets could be obtained from St. Aubyns church. These could be hired for 2d a blanket, providing they were washed and dried on their return. Generally, people used their coats for extra warmth as bedding during winter.

As soon as spring emerged from the darkness of winter, the men would make their way to the allotments situated behind New Town. These had been prepared by felling trees and clearing the ground. Some of the trunks were used to re-inforce the old rickety bridge that spanned the 'ditch'. The allotments were so popular that more land was allocated on the other side of the ditch, and even more land nearer to Hermitage Road. When the building started in this area the allotments were moved to the waste ground by the side of the 'rec', and later moved again to Ryfield Road, by the side of the convent woods. They were always an unsightly feature but helped the families with the produce that was grown in the summer months.

Several of my uncles kept an allotment, and one Mr. Jack Edwards, met with a most grisly experience in about 1920. Whilst digging he struck a mysterious object, and upon further digging uncovered a brown paper bundle. Thinking that he had discovered some hidden treasure and feeling elated, his hopes were soon disillusioned, for, as he uncovered the brown paper the remains of a human leg was revealed. The leg was taken to the police station in Gipsy Hill, and after police investigation it was revealed that a young medical student had been using the leg for medical research, and not knowing what to do with it after he had finished the examination, buried it in the allotments. Another tale related to me, was that one chappie grew his broad beans in fish heads. No different to fertiliser used today, except the smell was so offensive that everyone steered clear away from the spot!

The fields all around New Town not only gave the children somewhere to play, but also produced blackberries for picking. Musto's field produced the best blackberries and this is where the children would go. Musto's field is where Ryfield Road is to-day. The children would pick blackberries for a pie for their favourite 'afters'. Many a time they would nearly have a dish full when someone would shout 'here comes the farmer and his dog', and in their fright they would drop the dish and run for their lives. This particular part is where the notice board saying 'trespassers will be prosecuted' was placed. In later years when my uncles became friendly with the farmer, he said he did not know why the children ran so fast, he could hardly move and the dog was nearly blind!

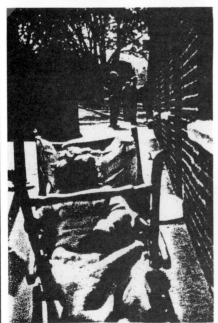

Top: An 'Oxford Arms' outing to Brighton c1920. Left to right back row: Harry Taylor, Bob Bromly, Fred Gee, George Brom. Front: Sid Bromly, Tom (Tiddler) Terry, Perce Harding, Ernie Biddle.
Left: The 'Gap' at the end of 'Little' Eagle Hill with Roy Fisher in the pushchair.
Below: Em and Elsie Smith.

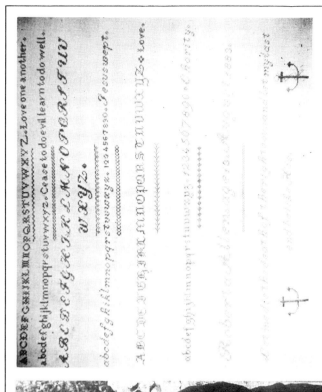

Left: The Wightman family in their garden in 17 Crystal Terrace which backed on to the Cottage Hospital. Left to right: back, Alf and George. Flo, Ted, Mrs. Wightman. Doll, Len and Grace.

Above: a sampler made by Mrs. R. Wightman when she was 13 years old.

Many of the large houses grew apple trees and the owners of Annadale, (situated in Roman Road,) would use the children to pick the apples. After careful picking they would then be allowed to pick up any apples that had fallen on the ground and take home as many as they could carry. The usual practice for children was to knock on the door of the houses and ask if they had any 'windfalls'; picking up the apples helped to keep the gardens tidy. There were many lads convicted at the juvenile courts quarter sessions, for stealing apples and pears.

Mr. Horace Margets remembers regularly going to Annadale to collect a dinner for his grandfather, who may have worked there in his earlier years.

Although money was scarce there were no real scruffy families, and everyone lived cleanly and dressed as best as they could especially for Sundays. Very few men would be seen without head gear, – trilby, bowler or a cap, and a white silk scarf adorning the throat. An heirloom watch chain would be proudly draped across the waistcoat and in the jacket, a flower displayed in the top buttonhole. Often on Sundays men would reminisce about past glories, and Mr. Charlie Johnson decked out in his Sunday best would proudly display his Boer war medals given to him for his valour.

The Sally Ann (Salvation Army) was a regular sight, assembling by a convenient focal point in the street. Children and onlookers would gather and join lustily with the choruses and hymns to the accompaniment of tambourines, accordions and other musical instruments. Sometimes a full blown band might assemble, complete with the base drum. Afterwards a collection box would be taken round to each house and even with the existing poverty, people then as now, always tried to make some donation, no matter how small. Everyone knew how good and kind the Salvation Army was to anyone who was in a less unfortunate position than they were.

Sunday was the day that everyone enjoyed. The mothers wore a clean starched white apron and the children all dressed in their Sunday best. It was always a special day, and anything that was an 'extra' during the week was kept until Sunday. In the afternoon the children would go to one of the two Sunday schools, where good attendance always meant an outing in the summer, and a tea party at Christmas – well worth looking forward to.

Sunday was generally the day for visitors, and uncles, aunts and cousins would call, bringing welcomed provisions for the afternoon tea. On the table, a large bowl of watercress was always to be seen, and maybe also some shellfish if money was available. The day generally ended up with a musical evening and the whole family joined in, enjoying a closeness that is lost to most families to-day. The majority of the musical instruments would be of a simple nature, such as clicking bones, spoons, and silver paper with a comb, but mouth organs and accordions were the most popular. As extra money became available, a pianola would be brought, which took pride of place in the home.

Perhaps someone would be fortunate to possess a packet of 'fags' and these would be handed around. A packet of Woodbine cigarettes in the twentieth century could be bought for 5 for 2d or Nosegay tobacco made up into home made 'fags'.

Rhyming ditties seemed to be a firm favourite, some hardly had any tune, none of them made sense, yet people would all sing and laugh as they were singing:

Carolina Pink, she fell down the sink,
She caught the scarlet fever,
Her old man had to leave 'er,
In came Doctor Blue,
He caught it too,
Carolina Pink from China Town.

Even Christmas produced its mirth and merriment. Sprigs of holly and home made decorations would transform the drab houses into a fairyland palace. A piece of yew for a Christmas tree, decorated with baubles and brightly covered wrapped chocolates brought from Mr. Tiegen's Christmas club. The ever longed for Christmas stocking would be hung up. Not that the items ever changed, a shiny new penny; an apple; an orange; a few sweets, and a new handmade pinny. But it still added to the excitement of a Christmas morning and brought pleasure and happiness into the lives of the children.

Remembered by many people were the bells of St. Leonards, Streatham, pealing out their goodwill chimes to welcome in the New Year. Families would join up for this recognised event by standing on their doorsteps listening to this lovely sound.

Hearing the older generation speaking of these bad times, it is hard for us today to imagine just how tough life really was, yet they recall their memories with love, and each relate their tales in a humorous way.

UPPER NORWOOD.

CHRISTMAS CAROLS.—As it is some time) since Christmas in Upper Norwood has been heralded in the good old-fashioned way —by singing carols, we were much pleased on passing through Church-road on Tuesday evening, by hearing a well-trained body of voices performing there. On making enquiries we found they were a choir of boys, assisted by a few gentlemen of All Saints' choir, serenading the Vicar, churchwardens, and some of the members of the congregation resident in the neighbourhood. We cannot help remarking the vigour and tunefulness with which the boys sang, which fact reflects great credit on Mr. Thornton, the schoolmaster at the National schools, who has trained them to such a degree of proficiency.

December 28th 1872.

83

CHAPTER TEN

LIFE & DEATH

Nothing changes throughout all centuries, life and death prevail, bringing gladness, suffering and sadness to everyone. Each generation makes room for the next, some enjoying a good life, others struggling just to exist. A wedding was something everyone looked forward to as it always caused great excitement and was the topic of conversation for many days. People would stand at their gates to wish the bride every happiness. The saying that a bride must wear 'something old, something new, something borrowed, something blue,' always prevailed. At All Saints Church bells pealed out their tune, welcoming the happy wedding day of the bride and groom. Afterwards confetti would be thrown, and the happy couple celebrated the wedding reception in their own home. If the wedding was at St. Margaret's church, the couple generally walked to the event. Not many of the New Town women started married life in their own home and usually had to make do with a couple of rooms in their parents' house, or someone's house along the road.

Without birth control families were very large and the women were usually pregnant nearly every two years. Old wives tales were handed down from mother to daughter. The ever faithful gin and epsom salts, hot baths, and a visit to a herbal shop were recommended, anything to prevent another mouth to be fed. Families in New Town seemed to be on average, seven to eight children in a family. It was a constant worry to the women as they experienced one pregnancy after another. The back street practices of abortions cost many women their lives.

Infant mortality was quite high and with money being scarce, a baby would often be buried with someone else, permission being granted by the other family. The little white coffin would be put under the driver's seat as the horse and glass hearse made its way to the cemetery. More than one in ten babies born before 1914 died before they reached their first birthday. The main causes were diarrhoea, enteritis, bronchitis, pneumonia and wasting diseases. You have only to walk in the cemetery grounds to see how sad it was that so many young lives did not reach maturity.

Generally it was the women 'down the road' who came and helped with the confinement. Mrs. Kettle who lived in Rockmount Road, and the Widow Biddle (not to be confused with Mrs. Biddle), lived half way down Eagle Hill. The baby would be washed in the large china bowl that stood on the chest of drawers, and water would be to hand in the jug. Relatives and friends were soon visiting to view the new arrival, bringing some home-made cakes, bread pudding or a little gift for mother and infant.

The Midwife Act came into force in 1907, and all women connected with midwifery were enforced to register. There were many convictions, either because the birth was not registered, or because the women had not notified the authorities that she had helped with a confinement. Courses were now in operation for everyone in this nature of work, but old customs died hard. These women had been delivering babies all their lives, but now they were to come under the jurisdiction of the council.

Burials were always a grand affair, the men attired in black suits and the women wearing black hats with veils over the face called 'widows weeds'. It was the custom for showing your respect. The curtains would be drawn tightly in each house during the allotted time as the coffin passed by. Everyone stood still and the men removed their trilbys, bowlers or caps. For months later in mourning the family wore a black cloth band or small black diamond shape sewn to their coat. Printed funeral cards would be sent out to relatives and friends, stating the date of the deceased with a small memorial verse.

On average, life expectancy in these early years of the twentieth century was 52 for males and 55 for females. Common grave charges were approximately 15/- adults and 12/- children.

Although money was scarce, everything was done in style and most people managed to find money for a burial. At certain times however, when there was no money available, the deceased would be buried in what was known as a 'paupers' grave. These graves would sometimes hold as many as seven or eight coffins, one on top of the other. Each had their own memorial stone and each was tended with just as much loving care.

A collection in the road was a recognised custom in respect of the deceased. A wreath would be bought – price between 5/- & 15/- and the remainder of the contributions handed over to the family. If it was the bread winner of the family, then any donations would be very gratefully received by the wife.

Most people were insured with The Prudential Insurance Co. When a baby was born it was a recognised fact that you took out a penny death insurance. Although this does not seem very much today it was quite a lot of money for families to pay out, but it did help with a death in the family. Often the insurance premium would get into arrears and then a little extra money each week would have to be paid to make up the deficiency.

The Gipsy Hill and Upper Norwood dispensary, was established to provide the working classes with efficient medicine and surgical attendance at a weekly charge, the deficiency being defrayed by charitable contributions.

To the Editor of the *Norwood News*. An extract from Correspondence column – March 16th 1878

Sir, There is an institution in Upper Norwood doing quietly and well, a kindly and useful work whose existence seems to be known but for a few, and which is now in need of more hearty support than it has lately been receiving. I refer to 'the Gipsy Hill & Upper Norwood Dispensary' which was established in 1868 and which during the ten years that has elapsed, has relieved much suffering, softened much anxiety and has formed an excellent channel for the flow of charity benevolence. The object of the institution is to provide medical aid for the poor at a cost that shall not be burdensome to them – the plan is to receive small weekly contributions of a penny or more from those who enter themselves as members, who thus become entitled to the benefits of the society. These contributions assisted by the donations of subscribers form a fund from which the medical gentleman who attend the patients receive a moderate fee. Our excellent treasurer James Bell Esq., of Fox Lane will be happy to receive your subscriptions AND furnish information as will also, Your obedient servant

E. Pritchard Hon. Sec. Tudor Road.

During the year 1893, over 3000 people were treated. Doctors in attendance were Dr. Sharman, Dr. Maitland and Dr. De'Estere.

1911 saw a very much welcomed National Insurance Act. Workmen were deducted 2p week from their pay, the employer paid 1d and the government 1d. The money went into a central fund which paid for a sick worker to receive medical attention, and a weekly allowance.

Dr. De'Estere drove to his patients in an open top carriage looking very regal in his top hat. He charged 2/6d for each visit, but for consultation at the surgery the charge was 1/-. A doctor seen regularly in New Town was Dr. J.E. Bates, called by the local people 'Jelly Bates'. He was often seen walking through New Town hands clasped behind his back with his top hat perched on his head. It has been said that he was a little eccentric, but most people agreed that he was a very caring doctor and could say nothing bad about him. Another regular doctor to New Town, was Dr. Swain, who rode a bicycle to visit his patients.

The main hospital was the Waddon Isolation hospital. The horse found New Town hard going when pulling the ambulance up the hills. Most of the time it kept slipping back and the occupants inside wondered whether they were going to slide out of the rear door. It was a regular sight to see everyone pushing the carts up the hills, many convictions were found of cruelty to the poor horses. Epidemics of scarlet fever and diphtheria saw many children taken to Waddon hospital. The house would be fumigated throughout by lighting sulphur candles which helped kill off any germs still lurking about. Because of the various epidemics, sanitary inspectors made regular visits, New Town on the whole was quite clean compared to other places, and only one conviction was found during the period searched.

CHAPTER ELEVEN

YOUNG LIVES

Children then, as to-day, made the best of what they had, and except for feeling hungry most of the time, they made their own happiness. Pleasures were simple and enjoyment with laughter and a few kind words from someone made life worthwhile. The children hated the freezing cold weather and with the flimsy clothes that they wore would put on anything to keep out the cold. Most of the clothes were cast offs from someone they knew or the jumble sales at the missions. Nothing ever fitted but whatever you could get into you wore.

Mending of garments was regularly carried out; socks and stockings would be re-footed from those past darning, and the collars of mens' shirts would be turned inside out. The girls learnt to sew, darn and mend at an early age helping their mothers rectify clothing for their smaller brothers and sisters.

Both girls and boys wore boots which were usually the worse for wear, and quite often their feet would get wet. My uncle Tom told me that once he had saved up 2/6d from running errands. It had taken him a long time and he had saved every 'fadger', going without sweets to try and make savings. Eventually his boots had worn right through and he had to use his well earned savings to buy new boots!

When the children's errands had been run and their special jobs all completed, it was time for play. The children's games were relatively simple and consisted of the usual ball games, leap frog (jumping over one another), flying kites, improvised cricket with a lamp post for the wicket! Diablo, marbles, fag cards, hop scotch, whips & tops, dabs, conkers, steel hoops and skipping. When a hoop broke the children would take it to Mr. Smith who worked in the forge at Westow Hill. It could be mended for one penny.

There were many skipping songs sung to various ditties, one favourite was:

Half a pint of porter,
Penny on the can,
Hop, skip and back again,
If you can.

No doubt this song was handed down through the generations, when the evening jug of beer could be obtained from the 'jug & bottle' by a side entrance to the public house. The porter was all the dregs of beer that had overflowed from the hand pump into a receptacle below and was much cheaper to buy.

A great many games were made up by the children themselves. One was called 'Pin prick'. All they did was cut up pretty pictures from old books or cards that someone had given them. These were put between the leaves of a book then each child would have a turn with a pin. If they put the pin between the leaves where a picture was, the reward was the picture. Without expensive toys a pretty picture was something to be treasured. Another game was called 'Frog in the Hole'. Two children played, each had a piece of wood or stick plus a smaller piece of wood which was the ball. A well was made with a coat or similar clothing and the idea was to 'chip' the wood into the hole.

It is hard to visualise children playing in the streets today, but without cars the street was the children's playground. The older children could climb the garden wall over to the open ground and fields, helped by the boys who built up steps to make it easier for them all to play in the ever popular 'ditch', but the smaller children played close to the houses. If someone found two wheels it would make a scooter with a few bits of wood and if four wheels were found, an elaborate trolley could be made! Wooden stilts were also a favourite with the young boys as of course was the favourite 'knocking down ginger' – knocking on doors and running away much to the annoyance of the householders. In the winter, toffee tins obtained from 'Jacks shop' were used for sledges and what noise they must have made!

One of the New Town lads was 'Bruv' – not the brightest of children and then as now children were very cruel to someone not as bright as themselves. During this time policemen were very much respected and the majority of children lived in awe of the law. When 'Bruv' tried to join in with the boys, they would shout 'here comes a policemen' and poor Bruv would be terrified and run home as fast as he could.

Sometimes there would be a magic lantern show at the mission or, for a copper, you could visit The Electra Picture Palace in Westow Hill, commonly called Ike's. The films were silent and in black and white, many were comedies with Charlie Chaplin and Buster Keaton. A pianist played suitable music as an accompaniment to the film.

There were many attractions at the Crystal Palace and entrance to the band festivals could be gained by a 'boot polish tin lid' – a good sales gimmick! You can just imagine the children worrying their mothers to buy a tin of Cherry Blossom boot polish for 2d, or Nugget polish for 1d. On some special events, samples would be given out and everyone would try to visit the Crystal Palace on these occasions. A firm favourite with the children was the fair where you could enjoy a long time on the swings, especially if you knew someone from New Town who was in charge!

Meandering through the fields from Beulah Hill was yet another small babbling brook which eventually disappeared into a marshy piece of ground. A favourite pastime of the local lads was constructing a dam with stones whenever the flow was sufficient to create a small pond, much to the consternation of Mr. Freeman and the cows that grazed there. The boys always imagined themselves cowboys and tried to ride the poor cows! The lads were also fond of catching tiddlers from the well remembered 'Conkernero' pond, which stood alongside the public house, correctly called 'The Conquering Hero', in Beaulah Hill.

The few comics that were able to be bought were swapped between the families, well tattered and torn, but the bargaining still carried on at the door step. 'Comic Cuts' was one of the first to be published and it was everyone's favourite. You had great bargaining power with this comic. Other comics were 'Chips', 'Lots of Fun', 'Boys Own paper', 'Chums',

Hiding in the den.

'Jet Boys Friend'. The boys liked reading the comics together and would try and find a 'den'. One place being underneath the cellar in one of the boy's houses. It was very dark and they read by the light of a candle. There was no floor covering and when the mother was sweeping the floor above, all the dust and dirt would fall down on them!

On the 4th November a 'Guy Fox' would be made in remembrance of Mr. Guy Fawkes who tried unsuccessfully to blow up the houses of Parliament. 'Guy Fox' was a dummy made up from old clothes and stuffed with leaves, rags and paper. It would be displayed in an old pram or trolley in the hope that a few pennies would be dropped in the hat to enable the children to buy fireworks for Guy Fawkes night. In the gardens a bonfire would be lit and the evening of fireworks, together with sticky toffee and roasted chestnuts ended with the 'guy' being placed on the fire and all around clapped and sung:

Guy, Guy, stick him up high,
Hang him on a lamp post,
and then let him die.

Mr. George Jeffery drove a coach for the Brixton Orange Coach Station and the boys would climb aboard for a ride up to the top of Oxford Road. Mr. Bennet, the chief mechanic for the West Norwood Bus Garage, also gave the boys a ride. Thursday afternoons was a day everyone looked forward to for this was the day for the delivery of beer by Huggins Brewery. The barrels were delivered to 'The Oxford Arms' by a Foden Steam Engine, which caused a great deal of excitement as previously deliveries were made by horse and cart. The door hatches in the pavement would open and the boys watched the empty barrels being replaced by full beer barrels. The whole operation was carried out by ladder and rope, rolling the barrels into the cellar. After the work was completed a dozen boys or so would try and get on the back of the wagon as it made its way out of New Town.

As the boys grew into teenage lads, gambling fever became an obsession with them. The police were always patrolling the area knowing the haunts of the gamblers, but the boys, to try and outwit the police, would keep changing their 'den'. Sometimes it would be at the 'gap', another time on the 'rec', but when they found there was no escape they reverted to a tree house in the woods. Mostly the gambling was 'Pitch & Toss' or 'Banker' and afterwards they would end the episode of gambling in Jack's shop for a raspberry, lemon or strawberry hot drink and a piece of sponge cake (size about 4"x2"), this had icing on the top and cost a penny a slice. The cake was made by the Far Famed Cake Company. Everyone said how terrible the cake was, but it was still eaten with relish!

CHAPTER TWELVE

SHADOWS OF WAR

In this era, before the advent of modern day communications, people relied solely on word of mouth and newspapers; very few people were able to afford crystal sets. The disastrous events of the first world war are well documented in history books, but one tends to forget the upheaval it caused to the women and children. Memories today are still as vivid as they were yesterday.

Several weeks after the outbreak of war, the government, fearing Zeppelin raids ordered street lamps to be dimmed. These were mostly gas lights so the top part was painted black. When any aircraft or Zeppelins (an enormous gas filled airship) were seen approaching, a maroon siren screamed out a warning or a policeman came round on his bike. When all was safe the same procedure would be repeated.

Recruitment centres were everywhere and many a young man was quick to answer the call of duty to defend his country. It was a time of immense patriotic feelings and high ideals. Military bands helped with the recruitment and young children fell in beside them, banging improvised drums from saucepans. Military uniforms were a regular sight. The centres were ready to enlist any male who applied, sometimes turning a blind eye to those they knew were lying about their age. The recruiting age was 19 – 41 years.

Medical examinations were carried out on all males accepted, but four out of ten of the men were considered unfit for military service. The response to the recruiting drive was so great that most of the men trained in their civvy suits until uniforms could be provided for them. There were no rifles and sticks were used to improvise.

During the period of the first world war the Crystal Palace was closed to the public and was occupied by the Admiralty. The building was now officially called H.M.S Crystal Palace. During these five years it was a naval depot and more than 150,000 men of the Royal Naval Division were trained there. Many New Town people were employed by the various catering firms ministering to the above.

The young men of New Town were all too keen to enlist. Many were too young and wished that they were a few years older. One like my uncle nearly did succeed. In 1915, My uncle Tom Terry tried to join up at various places as all his 'mates' had enlisted. Finally, he managed to join up at the Strand, London, by saying that he was 16 years at the time. He spent three months training for the RND at the Crystal Palace, then he was drafted to Blandford, a military camp in Dorset to finish training on the rifle range.

When the drafts were ready for them to be sent to the Dardenelles, fifty were selected. After they had been cross examined it was soon discovered that young Tom had lied about his age and was discharged. Not to be daunted, he tried again in 1917 and joined the RNVR, the Royal Navy Volunteer Reserves. After six months training at Portsmouth, he ended the war in the Dover patrol. This was the coastal command looking out for mines, torpedoes etc.,

A few names of the New Town men who fought in the Great War:

Jim Stevens Jnr., Harry Bray, Sidney Stevens, Frederick Moyler, Arthur Jingle, Charles Jones, Steven Hockham, Richard Paul, Alfred Gibbs, James Terry, James Gibbs, Thomas Terry, Harry Gibbs, William Terry, Ernie Harvey, Frank Gibbs, Frank Geary, Robert Fenton Cornish, Joseph Bray, Francis Henry Martin, William Collingham Bromley, Ernest Smith, Sidney Smith, Wally Smith, Alfred Smith, Harry Smith, Joseph Townsend, D. Tompkins, Thomas Townsend.

There was disappointment for those who enjoyed football matches, as after Cup Final day, April 24th 1915, football matches were abandoned until the war ended. Rugby matches had stopped at the beginning, but horse racing was allowed to continue. It was also illegal to buy a round of drinks and exact measures in glasses were strictly adhered to. Food was becoming exceedingly scarce and by 1917 the Women's Land Army came into existence. The first commodity to be rationed was sugar, quickly followed by all other foods and in February 1918 a full rationing scheme commenced. Everyone tried to help the war effort with collections of newspapers, tins etc., and the Boy Scouts took over the control of this effort.

Many songs were published relevant to the war years and a few are listed here:

Keep the Home Fires Burning, Sister Susie's Sewing Shirts for Soldiers, Roses of Picardy, Under the Bridges of Paris, God Send You Back to Me, Pack up your Troubles, When the Beer is on the Table, If You Were the Only Girl in the World, Over There, Over There, How you Gonna Keep them Down on the Farm?, Good by-ee, Don't cry-ee, There's a Long Long Trail Awinding, Take Me Back to Dear Old Blighty, Roses of No-mans land, She'd say Comme Pronze Vous Papa, It's a Long Way to Tipperary, Mademoiselle from Armentiers.

A memory that was mentioned several times was how proud New Town was of one of the 'lads' Joseph Townsend who achieved the rank of 2nd Lt. in the 5th Battalion of the North Staffordshire Regiment. Regrettably he was one of the many casualties killed in action on the 2nd March 1918 defending the village of Bullecourt. The regiment was defending the village during the last offensive of the war, 539 men and 22 officers lost their lives. Sadly Mrs. Townsend lost two sons in the war, Joseph above and his brother Thomas.

Joseph Townsend,
2nd Lt. North
Staffordshire
Regiment.
Killed in action,
21st March 1918.

Many sad tales are told of escapades during wartime, but sometimes nice things do happen. The five Smith boys although of different regiments and scattered in different parts of the world, all eventually met up in France and came home safely.

The telegraph boy cycling into New Town put fear into everyone's hearts. It was an unpleasant task delivering the sad news of a death. The telegram would say 'Lord Kitchener sends his sympathy, and regrets to inform you etc., etc. Upon Lord Kitchener's death in 1916, the Army Council expressed its sympathy instead. New Town was comparatively lucky in having a low percentage of deaths. Out of forty or so men, only about ten are known to have lost their lives.

No one had expected the war to go on for so long, but when the end came, it happened very quickly. The death toll had been enormous, and it was to everyone's relief when the maroons and sirens sounded to announce that the war had ended. The church bells joined in, pealing out the joyful news. They had been dark days, but now everyone was jubilant and there were celebrations everywhere. People danced and sang in the streets and many

Nell Terry, Land Army Girl.

schools enjoyed a half day's holiday. Union Jacks were everywhere, flying from the windows, and children waved them around in all their glory. There were many processions arranged for celebration and firework displays were very prominent.

Memorials by public subscription were erected in towns and villages. A board commemorating those who had lost their lives was installed in Rockmount School as well as the plaque in the Cottage Hospital. Suggestions were made for a memorial to be erected on the Recreation ground but instead the location was changed to the front of St. Margaret's church.

NORWOOD NEWS January 20th 1920.

UPPER NORWOOD WAR MEMORIAL

Those associated with St. Margarets Church, Upper Norwood erected to the memory of thirty men connected with the church, who fell in the war, a cross in Portland stone on the land adjoining the church. It was dedicated on Sunday morning by Canon Taylor, vicar of All Saints who gave the address. A procession was formed from the church, consisting of the choir and clergy, Canon Taylor and Rev. H.M. Marshall, who is priest in charge of St. Margaret's. The proceedings aroused sympathetic interest in the neighbourhood, and many attended what was an impressive little ceremony.

After the war, silence was always observed in memory of those who had lost their lives. On November 11th, at 11am guns boomed out in Hyde Park, which marked the commencement of a two minute silence. Traffic came to a halt and everyone stood still remembering the tragic losses of the war. The end of the silence was broken by another salvo of guns, traffic resumed and people carried on as normal. It was a way of paying your own respects to the dead.

Top left: left to right, Jim Terry, Thomas Terry and Alf Gibbs.
Top right: Jack Edwards c1915. He organised dances, chess and whist drives at St. Margarets Mission Hall.
Below: Employees of the Lyons Cafeteria and sailors of the Naval Division at Crystal Palace c1915.

95

Before the war, Mr. Hance the shoemaker hung a card in his window showing the charges as 3/6d for men's boots and 2/9d for ladies' shoes. During the war he was fortunate to work on munitions for the Woolwich Arsenal and after the war he shared his extra income with his friends. He brought a piano and supplied drinks for the end of the war celebrations, his door always open until the money ran out. Then Mr. Hance put the cards back in the window and carried on as though nothing had happened. But this was the character that so many of the New Town people possessed. Mr. Hance had brought a lot of pleasure into everyone's dull life and he was rewarded by his own sense of satisfaction. Not for him the greed of 'I have more than you Jack'; he shared his good fortune with all those around him and his goodwill guesture was never forgotten.

It is a sad fact that war brings work for the unemployed and during the war years conditions for the working class slightly improved. People were employed on the munitions, military pay and rationing, but with the end of the war, unemployment by 1921 was just as bad again. Two million men were looking for work and wounded men were a regular sight standing on street corners selling matches, with a placard hung around their necks saying 'Ex serviceman'.

The depression continued well into 1933 when the number of unemployed totalled three million. At the Penge Labour exchange the queue was so long that the men lined up four abreast to draw their dole money.

Policemen firing the maroons that signalled an air attack or the all-clear.

96

CHAPTER THIRTEEN

END OF AN ERA

This early century is another world to that we know today. In writing this book, I may have referred more to my family's accounts than I intended. However, they are first hand experiences, and without their accounts, I doubt if I would have attempted such a task. Their day-to-day experiences were not isolated. They reflected the aspirations of any other working class family who lived through this difficult period of time.

Those who lived through this sad period of time and knew the pain of hunger at first hand, can relate their tales of the good times along with the bad. Very few would like to live through those hard times again.

Many notable people in the vicinity did all that they could to help the poorer families and it was only by donations and contributions from these that so much extra could be done.

In the beginning the controversial wall which had been met with so much disapproval, had now became a unique part of New Town. But in 1930, much to the dismay of the inhabitants the time had come for the wall to be demolished. They were seeing the urban sprawl swallow up the surrounding open land that had existed at the turn of the century. The ever present 'ditch' was gradually disappearing under the influx of a housing development in Hancock Road. This rapid expansion of housing, with trees being felled and ground being cleared at an alarming rate, was not welcomed by New Town people, but in the interest of people, progress must be made.

The earlier inhabitants are long gone, but a few of the later generation are still living and can remember the character of New Town. The gossip of women relating the tales of each household made New Town what it was, a close community, everyone knowing their neighbour, yet to-day all are strangers. The closeness has gone and the sharing and caring is only a memory.

The saying is that behind every good man there is a good woman, which generally applies to those that have succeeded in an achievement. This must surely also apply to the women of New Town, for without their endurance of hard domestic work, the families would not have survived. Each woman recognised her own attributes, no matter how small. The Christian virtues of hard work, honesty, thrift and priority of values were handed down to her children.

Sadly, the New Town that was, is now no more, the familiar shops and dwellings have made way for the new. 1967 saw the last of these old buildings being demolished.

There are only a few survivors of those bygone days; the oldest being the original oak tree, one of the pair that stood in the 'undeclared public highway' later called Hermitage Road, still standing as a silent testament to all that has gone. Another lone survivor standing in the playground of Rockmount school, is one of the willow trees that stood by the well known 'gap'; its roots extending down into the remaining silt of the old watercourse that once flowed through. A glimpse of the wall can still be seen at the back of the hospital grounds, Rockmount Road, and Crystal Terrace gardens, finally, the last two buildings built by Mr. Norris, remain at the top of Oxford Road. They are survivors against all odds and just a little reminder of all that has passed.

The ghosts of New Town are at rest, yet not forgotten, for without memories there is nothing.

Beryl D. Cheeseman 1991.

Maisie, Winnie and Edward Geary, c1910.

Dover Road in 1960.
Eagle Hill.

The last remaining two houses in Oxford Road, built around 1910.

APPENDICES

APPENDIX 1

DISCONTENTED

To the Editor of the *Norwood News*.

Sir, I trust to your well known sense of justice and fair play to give me an opportunity as a lease holder and ratepayer of New Town, of stating how that long suffering neighbourhood has been served by Mr. Bird and other speculating builders.

When I first commenced business in New Town about fourteen years ago and we had outlets to Beulah Hill and Central Hill, but an enterprising builder some six or seven years ago succeeded in depriving us of the right of way to Beulah Hill and we had to be content with a vague promise that we should have another outlet in place of the one we had lost.

When Rockmount School was made at the rate-payer's expense, we thought we had reached the end of our imprisonment, as the road was brought to within a dozen yards of our doors. But Mr. Bird soon dispelled our hopes by building a concrete wall ten feet high across the end of the road, so as to shut of the humble cottages at the bottom of New Town from the view of his tenants and also to prevent the inhabitants of those cottages from profaning Rockmount Road by passing through it.

He then gave the school board the piece of land next to the wall, in which to build a school, thinking they would make the entrance into New Town, but as by doing so they would be trespassing on freehold property his little scheme has miscarried and now the matter stands thus. If Mr. Bird will allow the inhabitants of New Town an outlet into Rockmount school, the owners of the freehold will consent to the school entrance being made on to their property and will be willing to put up with the nuisance of the occassion, but if Mr. Bird remains obstinate

there is no alternative but to make the entrance on the Rockmount Road.

Mr. Bird makes a whining appeal to the local Board, and the public for sympathy, but it seems to me that he is only reaping the reward of his own selfish conduct in shutting up the householders of New Town in a kind of sack, putting them to great inconvenience and seriously affecting business and property of all kinds.

By inserting this you will give the public an opportunity of judging as to how the matter really stands.

> *I remain, Dear Sir,*
> *Yours faithfully,*
> *W. Marsh*

The Fox under the Hill,
New Town,
Upper Norwood,
March 25th 1882

Sir, As the weeping, wailing, and gnashing of teeth type of letter, you graciously gave the impression last week, from the above, I may emphatically say go and tell this Fox that he has made a complete donkey of himself by writing to a newspaper a string of utterly absurd inaccuracies, and utter nonsense. Fox wails out that I have blocked up some rights of way which New Town held as their own, before the enterprising builder appeared there, as he says, nobody knows better than does the editor of the Norwood News to say nothing of the inhabitants of New Town itself, that there is no iota of truth in such a statement. New Town at this moment possesses all the rights of way that ever belonged to it. True, I built a wall and if instead one wall, I had chosen to build a dozen, they belong on my own land, who is to hinder and complain of my so doing, with any justice? Fox then goes on in his letter to perpetrate another fib, by saying that Rockmount Road was made at the rate-payer's cost, whilst any bricklayer's labourer occasionally on a visit to 'The Fox under the Hill' – presumably to ascertain the hour of the day and nothing more – could have given Fox the accurate information that newly constructed roads were always formed at the sole cost of the proprietors of the estate under development, and that sewers, roads, and paths were their first acts in such a procedure. As to my 'whining' as Fox says, I did in my letters, purposely to obtain sympathy, I do rather think the whining matter belongs more to Fox himself. "Foxes have holes" Fox complains that he is 'shut up in a hole' locally no doubt, but a hole is obviously a foxes proper allotment, therefore why does he complain, much more blame me for it? From the tone of Fox's letter, he evidently is not a nice old fox, so I leave him to whine or howl on with-out any further regard from

Sir, your obedient servant
E. Bird

Park House
South Norwood
March 29th 1882

Extract taken from the Norwood News.

In another column we publish a complaint from a correspondent at New Town. It is not clear that he lays the blame for the evils he suffers upon the right shoulders. The person in fault is the builder who built the houses in New Town, without taking care that proper means of access to them from all parts had been secured. If a man builds in the middle of a field because land is cheaper there, and secures no roads to his holding, neither he nor his tenants can afterwards blame those who buy the rest of the field which he had the opportunity of securing, if he had chosen to do so.

APPENDIX 2

CROYDON RATE BOOK NORWOOD
Situation of property in NEW TOWN

YEAR 1860	Name of Occupier	Name of Owner	Description of Property rates
2225	Henry Gilingham	Same	3 Houses
2257	Sheldrick	"	2 houses
2259	Wm. Woods	"	6 cottages
2336	Martins (Crook)	"	House
2336	" (Kileen)	"	"
2370	Rev.L. Abraham	Roper	"
2371	J. Roper	"	"
2372	Mr. Taylor	Sheldrick	House & Shop
2373	"	"	House
2374	Mr. Tyler	Same	"
2375	Mr. Clapham	Same	5 Houses
2376	J. Warren	Same	House
"	"	"	10 Cottages
"	"	"	4 Cottages
2377	Virtue	Same	House
"	"	"	"
2378	Chas. Steele	Same	House
"	"	"	"
"	"	"	3 cottages
2379	Thos. Nash	Same	House
2380	J. Gee	Mr. Martin	House
"	"	"	"
2381	Henry Robinson	Mr. Martin	House
2382	Henry Carter	Mr. Carter	4 Houses
2383	W. Howard	Same	Cottage
"	"	"	2 Cottages
2384	Isaac Smith	Chamberlain	Public House
"	"	"	1 Cottage
2385	Chamberlain	Same	7 Cottages
2386	W. Self	Same	House
2387	Mr. King	Boulious	Bakers shop
2388	Bouluois	Same	9 houses
2389	Mr. Quilter	Same	4 houses
2390	Burge	Same	6 houses
2391	Pither	Quilter	House & Shop
2392	Chatham Bldg. Society	Same	3 houses
2393	"	"	2 Cottages
2394	T. Vinall	Same	House

YEAR 1866

	Name of Occupier	Name of Owner	Description of Property rates
4037	Baxter	Same	House
4037	"	"	"
4041	Rich. Stanford	"	"
4050	Chatham Bldg. Soc.	"	3 Houses
4063	Martin (Crook)	Martin	House
4063	Martin (Kileen)	"	2 Cottages
4102	Gillingham	"	3 Houses
4103	Thos. Raper	"	House
4104	"	"	"
4105	Abnett	"	Beer House
4107	Taylor	Sheldrake	House
4108	Harrison	Tyler	"
4109	Clapham,	Same	"
4110	Virtue	"	"
4111	Steel	"	"
"	"	"	"
4112	Thos. Nash	"	"
"	"	"	"
4113	G. Jee	Martin	"
4115	G. Clapham	Same	4 houses
4116	W.Howard	"	2 Cotts 15 & 16
4116	Radburn	Howard	3 Cottages
4117	Isaac Smith	Chamberlain	"
4118	J. Howard	Same	5 Cottages
4119	John Stevens	Boulouis	Baker Shop
4120	Boulois	Same	9 Cottages
4121	Quilter	Same	4 Cottages
4122	Burgess	Same	6 Cottages
4123	T. Pither	Quilter	House & Shop
4124	Mackenzie	–	2 Cottages
4125	Street	Same	2 Cottages

NORWOOD NEW TOWN.

Entering from Central Hill by

OXFORD ROAD.

Right | 2 Gillingham, Mr Henry, sen. 3 Paddon, Mr Edward
4 Ford, Mr William (*Ironmonger in London*)
Abraham, Rev. J. L, *Professor of Hebrew, Chaldee, Greek, &c.*

......
Raper, Mr James   Taylor, T., *Painter, Glazier, &*
Tyler, —, *Builder, &c.*—'Mount Cottage', *let furnished*
Taylor, Edward, *Cab and Fly Proprietor*
Dyke, Peter (gardener)...Mrs D., *Laundress*
Kiddell, Mrs Emma, *Laundress*   [*Albert Terrace opposite*

Right-hand side
{ 1 Clapham, Samuel, *Agent to* 'British Empire Life Office'
  2 Broderick, William (gardener)
  3 Privett, George—(Wesleyan Service on Sundays at 3)
  4 Mussett, Robert (gardener)
  5 Wood, William, *Hairdresser*

16 Fahey, Lawrence, *Boot and Shoe maker*

PROSPECT PLACE
Left
Brown, George (painter, &c.)
Coppard, Thomas (carpenter)
Simpkin, George (glazier, &c.)

Turn on the right into CRYSTAL TERRACE
Hollman, R....Mrs H., *Tailoress*   Squirrell, S....Mrs S. *Charwoman*
Fisher, William Kennet (waiter)   Clark, John (bricklayer)
Cross the street to No.
11 Suckling, Edward, *Poulterer*   10 Stone, E....Mrs S., *Laundress*
9 O'Connor, Patrick (gardener)   8 Ling, James, *Carman*
7 Page, George (gardener)   6 Sawyer, Frederick
5 Bowell, James (gardener)   4 Barnes, Willinm (baker)
3 Taylor, Elizabeth, *Laundress*   2 Salmon, Daniel, *Bootmaker*
1 Francis, James (porter at the Crystal Palace)
WOODBRIDGE { 1 Burrows, John (carpenter)...Mrs B., *Laundress*
PLACE { 2 Fanner, Mrs Isabella, *Laundress*

Vinall, John Thomas, *Gardener, &c.*

Return up Oxford Road—enter ALBERT TERRACE (South)
Grant, Ephraim, *dealer in Coals, Grocery, &c.*
Parks, Francis, *Builder*
Moist, Henry (waiter at the Queen's Hotel)
Upton, Miss Ann, *Dressmaker*
Graham, John
Nash, Thos. (employed at Crystal P.) Darling, — (employed at C. P.)

BARNARD'S } Jee, George (painter)
COTTAGES } Killeen, — (policeman at the Crystal Palace)
Crook, Mrs Eliza, *Mangling done*   Robinson, Henry, *Grocery, &c.*

Turn down the hill on the right-hand, to SPA NEW ROAD
Chamberlain, Wm., *Well-digger*   Dartnell, John
Street, W. (policeman at C.P.)   Gearing, Wm. (carpenter)
Hockham, William   Holland, Francis

Four } Wood, George........Hockham, Benjamin
Cottages} Holder, Joseph........Lee, James (bricklayer)
Returning up the hill
Carpenter, Charles (gardener)—'Howard's Cottage'
Stephens, John (gardener)   Mathews, T. (policeman at C. P.)
Hall, William (plasterer)   Archer, E., and Clark, James
Glanfield, Thomas   Self, William, *Gardener & Ground-worker*
Dover, Henry John, *Builder*
Court, George, *Plumber, Painter, &c.*
Wrenn, John (cow-keeper)   Fuchia, — (gardener)

Return to Albert Terrace
EAGLE TAVERN—Smith, Isaac, *licensed Victualler*

TRUSCOTT TERRACE
{ 1 Unoccupied   2 Tripp, Lowing (blacksmith at Crystal P.)
  3 Bright, Benjamin Charles, *Dyer, Scourer, &c.*
  4 Terry, — (employed at C.P.)   5 Chandler, D. (carpenter)
  6 Sawyer, Mrs Ruth   [*Cross the street to No.*
  7 Adams, Thomas   Chamberlain, Mrs Mary

Cross the opening to ALBERT TERRACE (North)
15 King, John, *Baker*   14 Dover, Thomas (bricklayer)
13 Pymble, Richard (carpenter)   12 Fenwick, Fredk (carpenter)
11 Taylor, Geo. Hy. (bricklayer)   10 Last, Hy. C. (whitesmith, &c.)
9 Chapman, Benjamin (plasterer)   8 Wright, George (blacksmith)
7 Court, George, sen. (carpenter)   6 Stevens, Richard (joiner)
5 Hales, Samuel (gas-fitter)
4 Penny, Henry, *Sexton at All Saints' Church*
3 Stevens, George (coachman)   2 Scarborough, T.(cook at C.P.)
1 Pither, Thomas W., *Butcher and Greengrocer*

Proceed further back up Oxford Road to ALBERT ROAD
6 Curtis, James (bricklayer)   5 Hurvey, Thomas (plumber)
4 Wort, John (cab-driver)   3 Smith, Benjamin (coachman)
2 Arnold, Fredk Wm. (carpenter)   1 Hooper, James (carpenter)

[END OF THE NORWOOD DISTRICT.]

UPPER NORWOOD.

ALBERT ROAD.

Approached from Oxford Road.

RIGHT SIDE.

OXFORD ARMS—Bromley, James W., *Licensed Victualler*
2 Grayson, Thomas
3 Karns, William
4 Ives, George, bricklayer
5 Smith, J.
6 Bergan, Mrs.
7 Warr, Henry
6 Andrews, H.
5 Johnson, Mrs.
4 Wort, Edwin
3 O'Brien, Mrs., *Laundress*
2 Arnold, Mrs.
1 Ellis, Charles

LEFT SIDE.

Collins, Charles, *Cab Proprietor*

OXFORD ROAD.

From Central Hill—no thoroughfare.

RIGHT SIDE.

1 Morgan, William

2 Johnson, Thomas
3 Simpkins, George, painter
4 Gillingham, —; Poole, Dr., *Dispensary*
5 Raper, Mr. Joseph
6 Raper, Miss
7 Tasker, Robert, *General Shop*
8 Kent, A. J.
9 Odle, William
Sycamore Cottage—
    Mussett, Robert, gardener
    Mussett, Mrs., *Laundress*
Prospect Place—
    1 Clapham, Samuel, *Insurance Agent*
    2 Hill, Absalom, *Bootmaker*
    3 Birch, R.
    4 Stanford, Edward, gardener
    5 Agambar, James, gardener
    6 Mencke, Alfred
        Return on opposite side.

Steele's Cottages—
    3 Newton, G.
    2 Meadows, J.
    1 Harvey, Henry
At bottom of Oxford Road no thoroughfare.

RIGHT SIDE.

Comfort Cottages—
    1 Martin, James
    2 Page, —
    3 Raven, Arthur, gardener
    4 Land, Thomas
            Cross to
Crystal Terrace—
    13 Osborne, Mrs.
    12 Cooper, John, gardener
    11 Smith, Mrs., *Laundress*
    10 Keable, John
     9 Bailey, Mrs.
     8 *Unoccupied*
     7 Day, Joseph
     6 Smith, Samuel
     5 Duneclift, Mrs., *Laundress*
     4 Hall, John, gardener
     3 Ranger, Mrs., *Laundress*
     2 Wood, G.
     1 Kitchener, Henry
Woodbridge Place—
    1 Joyce, Edwin, bootmaker
    2 Page, F.
MISSION ROOM.
Geary, James, Vineall Cottage

ALBERT TERRACE.

From Oxford Road and leading to Spa New
Road.—LEFT SIDE.

1 Last, Henry C., *Grocer*
2 Harvey, Charles W., bootmaker
3 Bullen, Edward, gardener
4 Mummings, R., bootmaker
5 Johnson, Walter
6 Rawson, Wm., carpenter
7 Court, George, carpenter
8 Houghton, Charles
9 Higham, Frederick
10 Smith, John
11 Granger, Walter
12 Hill, Charles
13 Jones, Charles
14 Dover, Thomas, bricklayer
15 Collier, Samuel, *Baker*
Stevenson's Cottages—
 1 Cahill, Patrick
 2 Johnson, John
 3 Bryant, John
 4 Rockingham, Thomas
 5 Burtenshaw, Henry
 6 Fisher, John
  Cross over and return.
Steel Terrace—
 3 Cutting, G., *Grocer*
 2 Price, John
Vincent Cottages—
 1 Haggarty, Mrs., *Laundress*
 2 Grimshaw, R.
Nash Cottages—
 1 Darling, G.
 2 Killum, John
Bernard Cottages—
 1 Gee, William
 2 Price, James
James's Cottages—
 1 Avery, Henry
 2 Andrews, C.
Cutting, C., *Grocer*
  Pass Spa New Road.
Truscott Terrace—
 1 THE EAGLE—Hayden, William
 2 Adams, Henry
 3 Terry, William
 4 Bryant, G.
 5 Johnson Thomas
 6 Bartlett, —
 7 Sawyer, William
  Cross over.
 8 Treman, Mrs.
 9 Chamberlain, Mrs.
 10 Houghton, Henry

SPA NEW ROAD.

From Oxford Road—no thoroughfare.
RIGHT SIDE.

Morton Cottages—
 1 Trice, Henry
 2 Westaway, William
Beulah Terrace—
 1 Jones, Edward
 2 Harvey, Edward, painter
 3 Cross, John James
 4 Read, R. W.
 5 Elphic, Robert
 6 Court, Mrs. C.
 7 Hempstead, J., gardener
 8 Tolly, James, carpenter
 9 Kitchen, William
Wood, Thomas
Hockham, William
Grayson, Thomas
Hockham, Benjamin
Holland, Francis
FOX UNDER THE HILL—Marsh, Wn
Wood's Cottages—
 1 Wood, Mrs.
 2 Beadle, Mrs.
 3 Terry, William
 4 Harris, William
 5 Jones, E.
 6 Byford, D.
 7 Holland, J.

108

OXFORD ROAD.
Map C 1.—U.N., S.E.
From Central Hill to Crystal Terrace.
LEFT SIDE.

1 Jee Miss	5 *Unoccupied*
3 Langridge W.	7 *Adams* William

RIGHT SIDE.

King E. J., Shirburn
Knivett John Charles, Aynho
2 Hutchinson Montague
4 Morrison William
6 Money Edward
8 Morgan William, *Coal Agent*
10 Keable Frederick J., *Builder*
12 Howe Harry
14 Gwyer H. J., *General Shop*
16 Godfrey William
18 Rockingham Thomas
20 Martin Robert
22 Mead Charles W., *Grocer*

24 Land Thomas	30 Sandford Thos. W.
26 Geary Edward	32 Matthews William
28 Martin Charles	34 Parish William

NASEBY ROAD.
Map C 1.—U.N., S.E.
From Oxford Road to Dover Road.
LEFT SIDE.

ST. MARGARET'S MISSION ROOM

1 Baldwin David	
3 Jones Charles	7 Willis Mrs.
Chipping Robert	9 Stevens John
5 Stevens James	11 Brown William

RIGHT SIDE.

2 OXFORD ARMS—Collett Robt. W., *Lic. Vic.*	
4 *Unoccupied*	
6 Cornish Robt. E.	14 Hale F.
8 Inman William	16 Land Arthur
Tyler Thomas	18 Sharp David
10 Conway Mrs.	20 *Unoccupied*
Clark H.	22 Bray E.
12 Bowers —	24 Collens William
Terry Walter	26 Hance J.. *Bootmkr.*

CRYSTAL TERRACE.
Map C 1.—U.N., S.E.
From Oxford Road.—No thoroughfare.
LEFT SIDE.

MISSION CHURCH
1 Lewcock William J.

2 Osborne Mrs.	5 Harvey Thomas C.
3 Gibbs Mrs.	6 Tolley W. H.
4 Jones Henry	7 Smith Ernest A.

8 Smith Frederick	12 Wood George
9 *Unoccupied*	13 Tolley George
10 Martin William	14 Sullivan Thomas
11 Grainger William	15 Archer John

Cross and return.

16 Gregory W.	18 Badger F.
17 Wightman Joseph	19 Linden Samuel

DOVER ROAD.
Map C 1.—U.N., S.E.
From Oxford Road.—LEFT SIDE.

1 Bashford John	17 Shepherd Harry
3 Harvey Chas. Wm.,	19 Read Thomas
Bootmaker	21 Townsend William
5 Johnson Mrs.	23 Hills Mrs.
7 Townsend Albert C.	25 Mead John F.
9 Lloyd Jesse	27 Mead Henry Geo.
11 Nettle George Jas.	29 Plumbley J.,
13 Champion William	*Confectioner*
15 Spurgeon George	

Pass Naseby Road.

31 Tietgen G. T.,	35 Woolhouse Wm.
Grocer	37 Alexandra Ernest
33 Simpson W.	

RIGHT SIDE.

2 Wilson C.,	14 Bull Joseph
Greengrocer	16 Townsend Mrs.
4 Geary Mrs.	18 Charlesworth Mrs.
6 Tomkins J.,	20 Chamberlain Mrs.
Decorator	22 Styles W. T.,
8 Stockdale S. J.	*Bootmaker*
10 Kent Arthur J. A.	24 Bromley F. J.,
12 Gingell William	*Grocer*

Pass Eagle Hill.

26 Harris Henry	32 Johnson John
26A Colrus E. H.	34 Terry James
28 Burrows Henry	36 Gibbs J. H.
30 Terry W.	38 Terry Thomas

EAGLE HILL.
Map C 1.—U.N., S.E.

From 24, Dover Road.—No thoroughfare.

LEFT SIDE.

1	Beckett Walter	27	Howard W. H.
3	Hockham Stephen	29	Searle Henry Wm.
5	Ewens Wm. James	31	*Unoccupied*
7	Hunt Chas. James	33	Brand Joseph,
9	Biddle William J.		*General Shop*
11	Terry Henry	35	Rockingham Wm.
13	*Unoccupied*	37	Moyler William
15	Carter Alfred	39	Hockham James
17	Tilley Bertram	41	Poole William
19	Durling Wm. Geo.	43	Wood Mrs.
21	Friend Henry	45	Wade William
23	Biddle Mrs.	47	Freeman Robert,
25	Simpson George		*Dealer*

RIGHT SIDE.

2	Hoare William	30	Chamberlain Wm.
4	Taylor F.	32	Drewett Mrs.
6	Gibbs John	34	Tester William
8	Bromley William	36	Farley Wm. John
10	Willsmore George	38	Johnson William J.
12	Allard Fredk.Chas.	40	Earley Albert Wm.
14	Bushell Ernest W.	42	Taylor Arthur
16	Sibbald John	44	Page H.
18	Nicholls Alfred	46	Bray George
20	Wilson Mrs.	48	*Unoccupied*
22	Hockham Stephen	50	Page William
24	Tyler Mrs.Caroline	52	Bray Mrs.
26	Rex Robert	54	Cummings Arthur
28	Terry William	56	*Unoccupied*

"Little' Eagle Hill.

110

APPENDIX 4

ROCKMOUNT SCHOOL
Admission Papers – 28th February 1883

FEES
2d for the first child & 1d for additional children. Exercise books 3d per annum for homework.

BOYS SCHOOL

Robert Reed	9
Albert Rawson	11
Edward Mates	9
Henry Mead	7
John Shepherd	9
Leonard Norris	8
Fred Edbrook	10
Robert Martin	8
George Roberts	7
Fred Jee	7
Fred Denton	9
Arthur Congram	7
Chas. Edbrook	10
Edw. Harvey	11
Alf. Edbrook	12
Cornelius Ranner	8
Henry Biddle	11
Walter Andrews	10
Wm.Hallett	11
Chas. Johnson	10
Walter Cross	11
Cornelius Land	8
William Smith	7
Fred Avery	11
Wm Houghton	8
Victor Fisher	8
George Johnson	8
Charles Ewen	10
Wm. Ives	9
Albert Ellis	8
Walter Johnson	10
Wm. Mountain	10
Fred Howard	8

James Dixon	9
Fred Ranner	13
Arthur Rockingham	8
Marshal Read	11
John Bold	12
George Mead	10
Stephen Knight	11
George Buck	13
Wm.Rockinghmam	10
Fred Bold	13
Wm.Reed	13
Thomas Mead	12
George McIver	12
Richard Wood	13
Wm.Kitchen	10
Thomas Roberts	14
George Wood	13
John McIver	10
Henry Raven	13
Fred Stidwell	11
George Morgan	14
Wm.Congram	13
Norman Roberts	12
Percy Bryant	13

GIRLS SCHOOL

Gertrude Dyer	8
Alice Vincent	8
Florence Birch	7
Elizabeth Mead	9
Minnie Westaway	8
Annie Roberts	10
Ethel Spackman	10
Frances Houghton	11
Annie Martin	10
Minnie Land	10
Annie "	7
Priscilla Browell	9
Louisa Willsmore	9
Minnie Dyer	9

Florence Gibbs	10
Minnie "	10
Ellen Biddle	12
Clare Starr	11
Florence Mitchell	11
Susan Harvey	7
Louisa Dee	8
Annie Elphick	9
Kate Howard	7
Rose Wood	12
Georgina Hedger	8
Louisa Denton	11
Rose Stevens	7
Mary Johnson	10
Ellen "	8
Alice "	10
Kate "	7
Alice Hockham	12
Mary Miles	12
Florence Trice	14
Agnes Bold	9
Jane Brocott	11
Maud Bartlett	11
Elizabeth Dee	12
Emma Bold	12
Alice Payne	12
Ella Scrimshaw	10
Evelyn Smith	10
Ellen Relf	10
Eleanor Martin	10
Louisa Johnson	10
Mary Birch	10
Charlotte Howard	11
Alice Hempstead	11
Isabel Morgan	11
Louisa Elfes	10
Harriett Pikes	10

Alice Mussett	11	George Hempstead	6
Alice Page	10	Minnie Johnson	5
		Herbert Howard	6
INFANT SCHOOL		Edith Fisher	5
Wallter How	4	Ellen Payne	4
Henry Dyer	6	Ruth Bartlett	6
Samuel Denton	5	Ben Johnson	6
Fred Johnson	5	John Johnson	6
George Scrimshaw	5	Herbert Johnson	6
Thomas Norris	4	Ellen Payne	4
Frank Martin	6	Ada Harris	5
Constance Johnson	6	Sarah Hance	6
Henry Johnson	6		
Wm.Chamberlain	6	**Names crossed out:**	
Annie Dee	5	Frederick Keble	4
Charles Mates	6	Ernest Seclure	5
Harry Rockingham	6	Elizabeth Geary	4
Edwin Smith	5	Wm. Edmondson	4
Herbert Martin	5	Harriett Holland	6
Alfred Brooks	5	Frank Edbrook	6
John Edmonson	5	George Browell	5
Edward Houghton	6	Julia Denton	4
Edward Jones 5			

APPENDIX 5

THE COTTAGE HOSPITAL
Interesting events taken from the minutes of The Cottage Hospital

1885 8th June
Monthly bills amounting to £74.12.10p – Purchase of a mattress for the operating table. New wall and repairs to roof.

1885 3rd Oct
Temporary closure due to illness of Matron and symptoms of diptheria at the hospital. Dr.Gandy proposed that during the disinfecting and whitewashing of the hospital, no fresh cases should be admitted.

1886 5th April
Endowment by Mrs. Eusden of a bed to be called 'Hokkaido' bed. Balance of donation to the Samaritan Convalescent & Seaside Fund, as it would assist the poor and destitute patients, and help to provide them with clothing.

1886 31st May
Grateful acknowledgement to Mr. Johnson & his son, Oxford Road, for valuable assistance to the matron and staff at all hours of the day and night.

1889 31st May 1.6.88 – 31.5.89
110 patients treated. 20 persons sent to the Samaritan Seaside Convalescent. The convalescent fund has been well supported, groceries, clothes, small donations of money, boots etc.,

1889 9th Dec
Donation for bed called Emperor Frederick William bed.

1898 10th Jan
Miss. E.J. Phillips first matron of the hospital appreciation of her work for fifteen years.

1907 8th Dec
Slight fire in the boiler room, quickly attended to by the South Norwood Fire Brigade.

1910 10th Oct
Transformer of the X-Ray apparatus broken down, discussion whether to buy new or the old one repaired.

1910 26th Oct
Mr. Simon Symons generously offered to give £100 for the new apparatus. Dr. Eccles (the Hon. Electrologist) submitted an estimate for supplying and fixing a new up-to-date X-Ray apparatus from Mr. Alfred E. Dean for the sum of £100. The committee accepted Mr. Simon Symons generous offer.

1911 11th Dec
Outbreak of scarlet fever – drains examined. Messrs. Bowyer to rectify defective portion of the damaged drain.

1912 12th Feb
Recommendation for throat & ear department.

The Norwood Cottage Hospital

A few memorial inscriptions originally located in the Norwood Cottage Hospital to those who had faithfully served the people, but now under the jurisdiction of the Clerk of the Works, Croydon.

Sited in the front door a beautiful stained glass:

> In memory to Henry Phillips who died 23rd October 1893 the first secretary of the hospital.

Close to the entrance a window filled in by design in stained glass, represented the Apostles Peter and John restoring the lame man at the Beautiful Gate of the Temple, it is surrounded by the following inscription:

> In memory of John Brockwell LRCP. HRCS., Surgeon of the hospital died June 1894

A handsome brass tablet:

> In memory of Major-General Robert Ranken, Madras Staff Corp. Honorary Treasuer of this hospital 1882-1895

An inscription to Doctor John Sharman MRCS died January 1890:

> To the memory of: Captain Robert Williamson Ramsey Late of the Black Watch Royal Highlanders Vice President 1887

A excellent tribute to Captain Robert Ramsey was found in the annual report of 1887 which I feel deserves a mention:

> Captain Ramsey entered into the

idea of forming a hospital at Norwood the moment it was suggested to him, continuing from that time to his death to take the warmest interest in its welfare. Every proposal for increasing its efficiency or extending its influence found in him a prompt and liberal friend. He gave not only material support but active personal help and warm sympathy to every plan for relieving the sick and destitute, whether connected with the Cottage Hospital or not. His spotless character, his generous sympathies, his courtly manner, ensured him the respect and attachment of all who knew him; and by them his name will long be mentioned with the reverence and affection which attend the memory of the just.

OBITUARY
1887 31st May.
James Watney Esq., MP., President of the hospital.

> Joseph Tritton Esq., Vice President. His death will be mourned by the sick and needy over a far wider area than that to which the operations of the Norwood Cottage Hospital extend.

Pax vobis. (Peace be unto you).

114

APPENDIX 6

Various events – NORWOOD REVIEW & CRYSTAL PALACE REPORTER

1869 Sept18th
Licence William A. Abnett of the Oxford Arms. Albert Road, Upper Norwood.

1869 Oct 23rd
Two Cottages to let in Crystal Terrace Apply Mr. Salmon in same terrace, or Mrs. Warren 130 Crown Hill, Croydon.

1871 Nov 18th
Notice has been served to repair roads in New Town.Upper Norwood.

1872 Feb 10th
Newspaper reports on condition of deplorable state of roads in New Town.

1872
A year of strikes.

1872 May 11th
Notice to be served on owners for repair of roads in New Town.

1880 May 15th
A boy attacked by a cow – about 10am Monday morning last as a cow and her calf, belonging to Mr. Grant, Dairy of 1 Hamilton Road, was being driven along Church Road, the animal ran and threw a little boy named Herbert Bryan of Truscott Terrace, New Town, four years old as he was walking with his sister. The little fellow was immediately taken to Mr. Primes the dentist, but only a slight fracture of the skin could be found. The boy was much frightened and we are pleased to he has completely recovered from the shock.

1882 August
Missing – On the night of Saturday three cows, two owned by Mr. French, Dairyman of Westow Hill and the other by Mr. Holliday of Norwood New Town, mysteriously disappeared from a field in Aukland Road, and have not since been heard of. Whether the animals were stolen or whether they they strayed, cannot be said, but the police have been unable, as yet, to trace their whereabouts. It is a very serious loss to the owners, the cows being valued at upwards of £70.

1885 August
Very high temperatures 87.

1885 November 28th
Mr. W.P. Morrison held an enquiry at The Oxford Arms into the circumstances attending the death of Susan Harrington, a married women residing in New Town, who met a fatal accident on Saturday evening, Mr. Munnings was chosen foreman; Charles Harrington 20 Oxford House, New Town stated that the dead woman was his late wife age 44 years – Verdict – too much to drink.

1886 February 13th
Demonstrations in London about the unemployed.

1886 February 20th
Letter to the editor about the unemployed working on the roads.

1886 March 13th
Procession of the unemployed.

1886 March 20th
Prevailing distress of the unemployed.

1886 August 28th
Mision Church New Town Rev. T.W. Bowen.

1886 November 6th
Something to be done about the unemployed in the shape of a free registry at Streatham.

1886
Soup kitchen by Miss. Leggett at Gipsy Hill.

1886 November 20th
An accident happened on Monday afternoon to a cart belonging to Mr. Rackstraw Biscuit Manfc., Chelsea. The horse was standing near Crystal Terrace, New Town when it bolted, the cart being overturned by coming into contact with the kerb, breaking panes of glass in Mr. Dunnicliffe's window. The animal's thigh was slightly grazed, but no damage was done to the cart.

1886 December 4th
Determined Suicide – Catherine Burrows wife of Charles Burrows. 10 Woods Cottages.

1887 January 8th
Skating on South Norwood Lake.

1887 January 15th
Procession of the unemployed.

1887 January 22nd
Procession of the unemployed.

1887 April 9th
Breakfast mornings being discontinued.

1887 April 30th
Archbishop of Canterbury preached in Norwood.

1887
Children's Jubilee treat – various places, Mr. Wood's meadow, Harold Road.

1899
Gales swept over the country & houses blown down.

19011
An Edwardian summer – An excess of bright sunshine.

1908
Old Age Pension Act 5/- per week for persons over 70 years of age, in receipt of incomes not exeeding 8/- per week.

19111June 24th
The feeding of children for Coronation Day celebrations.

1911 June 24th
Coronation of King George V & Queen Mary. The crowds in Upper Norwood maintained such commendable order on Thursday that not a single charge was recorded at the Gipsy Hill Police Station.

PETTY CRIMES

1878 August
Henry Hollands Tailor of New Town summoned for wilfully doing damage to the window of Thomas Dover on the 6th August. Defendant said he broke the window while throwing at a cat. Chairman ordered the defendant to pay 5s damage and 5s cost. Defendant asked for time. Mrs. Dover said she saw the defendant come out of The Eagle Public House, used some expression against her husband and threw a stone and run away. The damage done 3s, defendant said the glass was only worth a shilling. Elizabeth Marsh confirmed the statement of Mrs. Dover.

1878 August
Thomas Malarny of Laurel Cottage New Town charged with assaulting and threatening his wife Catherine. Mr. Eridge said that the parties had only

been married six months He now begged his wife's forgiveness. Fined £10.

1885 January 17th
Theft of coat Mr. Charles Bore Woods Cottages New Town.

1885 January 31st
Assaulting the Police Peter Sullivan labourer 2 Oxford Road, New Town. One months hard labour.

1885
Deserter from the Royal Marines Harry Gee alias William Henry Ware, New Town.

1885 August 8th
John Cross labourer charged at Croydon with assaulting two nursemaids by attempting to kiss them, whilst under the influence of drink in Hermitage Road. Prisoner guilty – Fined 10/- and 7/- costs.

1885 December 19th
Mr. Simmonds of Woods Cottages, New Town. Fined 5/-for being drunk & disorderly.

1886 March 6th
Harry Gee alias Harry Harvey, alias William Henry Ware age 22 a native of New Town and a deserter from the Royal Marines was indicted for obtaining a quantity of clothing from various parts of the metropolis by fraud. Pleaded guilty. 18 months hard labour.

1886 March 20th
George Burgin Bricklayer drunk and using bad language Fined 5/- 2/6d costs.

1886 September 18th
An assault charge Walter Grainger was summoned by David Pope for using insulting and threatening language to him. Fined 2/6d 9 Crystal Terrace, New Town.

1886
Robert Johnson charged with felony for entering Mr. Claphams house 12 Oxford Road. New Town.

1886 October 9th
William Biddle of New Town being in the unlawful possession of pears, in Central Hill. Fined 10/- or 7 days.

1886 October 16th
Theft of Fireworks. Arthur Court, Spa Road, New Town charged at Lambeth for stealing some fireworks value 2/6d property of Messrs. Brock's Firework Co., To come up for judgement if required.

1886 October 23rd
Henry Biddle an errand boy of Upper Norwood, stealing pears from a garden of the Hawthorns, Beaulah Hill. Value 5d Property of J. Relf – Remanded in workhouse – a week later discharged with caution and handed over in care of his mother. Belief that a week's detention would do him good.

1886 December 11th
Annie Biddle a young girl living at 1 Woods Cottages, New Town Drunk and incapable. Fined 1/-.

1887 April 2nd
Alleged impudent theft, New Town. John Goss hawker was charged with stealing a purse containing £1.6s.10d the property of Esther Dunecliffe of 2 Crystal Terrace, New Town. Prosecutrix stated that the prisoner and a woman came into the shop and asked to look at some children's clothing. Whilst she was on the stool, she felt a hand in her pocket. Prisoner passed out the door and she gave the alarm. Eliza Holton of 8 Albert Terrace, New Town stated that she saw the prisoner very agitated and she saw him throw something into Mrs .Johnson's backyard. Mrs. Johnson 1 Vincent Place, New Town, found the purse in her backyard. John Goss 3 months.

1889 November 9th

Frederick Thompson a dealer of Beaulah Hill, charged at Croydon on Thursday with having been drunk and incapable of taking care of a horse and cart in Hermitage Road on the previous day. Fined 5/- & 5/- costs.

1920 May 30th

William Cummings a lad of 54 Eagle Hill playing banker on Norwood Recreation ground. Placed on probation for two years. Getting on nicely at work, given another chance. Fined 2/6d costs.

1920

Sidney Tester 34 Eagle Hill age 17 playing banker earned 10/- per week. Bound over if he promised not to gamble again.

EXTRAORDINARY MISTAKE.—At the Lambeth police-court, on Tuesday, before Mr. Woolrych, *Bartholomew Charles Daley*, a corporal in the Lancers, was charged with breaking and entering a house in Albert-road, New Town, Norwood. The evidence was very lengthy, and from that it appeared the prisoner was in a few days to leave for Ireland, but before doing so, he resolved to pay his brother a visit, and accordingly repaired to his house, No. 3, Albert-road, Norwood, where he, and his brother, and a friend made so merry, that about an hour or so after midnight they all got into bed together in the back parlour, the prisoner being considerably the worse for drink. At something like three o'clock in the morning prisoner got up attired in his drawers and stockings, opened the front door, and went out into the street. He was (according to the statement of several parties) very much confused, and after wandering up the street came back as he thought, to his brother's house. Finding the door shut he opened the parlour window, got in, and proceeded to the back room, and got into bed. He had not been there very long before a woman in the bed called out, "Oh, my God, here's some man in the bed." This aroused the woman's husband, who at once started up and discovered the prisoner. He asked what business he had there, when he said he was a soldier and wanted his clothes. The husband told him he would soldier him, and was about to attack him with a thick stick, but was prevented by the wife, who advised that the police should be sent for, and the supposed burglar given into custody. This was done, when prisoner said he believed he had been brought there by some women, and robbed of his clothes, and then rambled on into some other statement, in which there seemed but little sense. After his removal to the station, he said he thought he was in his brother's house, and from other remarks he made Sergeant Tarrant, 4 P Reserve, went into Albert-road, and on coming to No. 3, he found the street door wide open. On entering the back room he saw two men in bed, who, on being aroused, proved to be the prisoner's brother and his friend, who seemed extremely surprised at prisoner's absence. On a chair in the room was the uniform of the prisoner.—Mr. Woolrych: This is a very singular charge, prisoner, What have you got to say to it?—Prisoner: The evidence is quite correct, but I never meant any harm. I got so confused with drink that I must have come out of my brother's house into the street instead of going into the yard, and on my return, believing the door had got shut, I made my way in at the window, believing it was my brother's house.—Sergt. Tarrant explained to his worship that the whole row of houses were of one appearance, and a mistake might be made by a stranger, particularly if his senses were not in the clearest state.—Mr. and Mrs. Tappington, the occupier of No. 1, said they had no desire to press the case, as they believed it was an unintentional affair.—The Prisoner, after receiving a severe lesson from Mr. Woolrych to abstain from drink, through which he had nearly been led into a very serious condition, was discharged, and he left the court with his friends.

APPENDIX 7

Obituaries

New Town residents:

1869 July 23rd Emma Martin age 2 years – 2 Albert Terrace. New Town.

1870 March 23rd Death of Mr. Edwin Holland, New Town.

1872 October 26th G. Gearing age 12 Claylands Cottage. New Town.

1877 February 17th Mrs. Emma Adams of 3 Truscott Terrace, New Town leaving 3 children surviving her.

1881 May 5th Henry Harvey age 24.

1885 July 17th Child suffocated – Enquiry held Eagle Public House. Body of infant three weeks Dommiccicco Guglimotte son of Dommiccicco & Catherine Amy Guglimotte 3 St. James Cottages, New Town.

1885 May 9th Amidst tokens of great respect the funeral of Mr. G. Darling to Croydon Cemetery. Following in the procession from New Town were many of the Crystal Palace company's staff, while the bearers consisted of those most intimate with the deceased Messrs. Hills, Wiseman, Runacre, Parker, Page and Evans. Among those who followed we noticed Messrs. Giddings, Bryant. Wilson, Wood, Bool, G. Scrimshaw and Casbourne. Several beautiful wreaths were sent contributed by Mr. Glass, Mr. G. Hill and others.

1885 November 31st Death of Mr. R. Scrimshaw age 71 an old resident of New Town for twenty years. The deceased was well known in the district and his more robust days, his pony and trolley used to be frequently seen at the entrance of the Crystal Palace, where the removal of carriages to and from the exhibition were entrusted in his care.

1886 May 1st Sudden death of an infant – Mrs. Tappenden residing at 2 Woods Cottages, New Town awoke at a quarter to six and discovered her infant Walter Henry Tappenden age 3 months dead at her side. Inquest being held.

1886 Oct 30th Death of Mrs. Haggerty – resided in New Town for many years. Died in the house of her son Mr. Norris.

1887 April 6th George Senior age 1 year.

1890 May 17th Samuel Clapham – age 89.

1892 April 22nd Jane Scrimshaw – age 68.

1898 Dec. 24th Sarah Elizabeth Clapham – age 82 Copthorne Churchyard.

1900 April 3rd Thomas Christopher Harvey – age 65.

1910 April 2nd Printer's death – Hand caught in machine. Mr. Hugh B. Jackson coroner for Croydon held an inquest on the body of Arthur Frederick Mathews, age 30 who died on Saturday last at Norwood Cottage Hospital. Mrs. Mary Ann Mathews mother of the deceased living at 32 Oxford Road, New Town, Upper Norwood. He was a printers machinist engaged at Mr. A.J. Squire's.

1920 Oct 1st Tragic suicide of lonely carpenter. Arthur Richard John Taylor age 47 of 12 Crystal Terrace, whose decomposed body was found 10 days after he died. He had been greatly worried since the death of his wife. Verdict – Whilst of unsound mind.

WORLD WAR I
NEW TOWN war casualties:

William Collingham Bromley L/Cpl Royal Fusiliers., Born New Town 12th December 1886 – Policeman – Enlisted 18th February 1904. Fell Somme 1st July 1916.

Robert Fenton Cornish Middlesex Regiment., Born Earlswood 4th March 1882. Married – Signwriter, 6 Naseby Road. Enlisted 14th August 1916. Fell Monchy le Preux 23rd April 1917. Buried Mil Cemetery between Heninel & Croisilles.

Francis Henry Martin Private RWS Reg. Born Eagle Hill, 18th Sept. 1876 Lather & Painter 7 Naseby Road, Enlisted 19th Nov. 1915. Somme July 1916. Died of wounds 12th October 1918.

Thomas George Mates RWS Reg., Resided 30 Eagle Hill, Shoemaker, 4th August 1914. Died 6th November 1914. German prisoner of War Hospital of wounds received at Ypres. Previous 13 years in Army.

James (Sacry) Alfred Stevens Private 10th October 1894 5 Naseby Road, Labourer. Enlisted 17th April 1916. Fell France 28th Sept. 1916.

Stephen Hockham Private 22 Eagle Hill Labourer residence 3 Eagle Hill, Enlisted September 1914. Died at home from Gas poisoning 25th August 1916.

William John Terry RWS Regiment., son of William & Charlotte Terry Born 17 Crystal Terrace, Lived 55 Eagle Hill. Enlisted 13th September 1910. Fell Ypres 21st October 1914.

Albert Tompkins Pte., E. Surrey Reg. 44 Eagle Hill 10th July 1891. Resided 6 Dover Road. Enlisted 10th August 1914. Fell France 14th May 1915.

Thomas Townsend resided Dover Road, New Town. Killed in action.

Joseph Townsend resided Dover Road, New Town. Killed in action 2nd March 1918.

In Memoriam.

APPENDIX 8

SHOP PROPRIETORS 1855-1930

Sarah Robinson	Grocer
Mr. J. King	Baker
Mr James North	Butcher
Benjamine Bloom	Grocer
S. Cooper	Bootmaker
D. Salmon	Bootmaker
Edward Taylor	Cab Proprieter
Lawrence Fahey	Boot & Shoemaker
Thomas Pither	Greengrocery & Butcher
Emphram Grant	Coal Merchant
John King	Baker
Henry Robinson	General Shop
Simon Cole	Boot & Shoemaker
Robert Tasker	General shop
James Darling	Grocer
Richard Wheatley	Baker
Jane Pither	General shop
John Stevens	Baker
G. Cutting	Grocer
John Leversuch	Cab & Fly Proprieter
Henry Last	Smith & Gas Fitter
Elizabeth Darling	Greengrocer
Robert Munnings	Boot & Shoemaker
Mrs Wiggen	General shop
Samuel Collier	Baker
Charles Townsend	Baker
Charles Collins	Cab Proprieter
Henry Longhurst	General shop
Haggar & Sorrel	Grocer
Mrs Henry Last	General shop
Robert Scrimshaw	General shop
James Price	Grocer
Mrs Dunnicliffe	Shop
Herbert Armitage	Greengrocer
William Higgins	Grocer
F.W.G. Hiller	Fishmonger
Thomas Williams	Cab Proprieter

William Henry Mead	Grocer
Misses Last	General shop
Sorrel & Talbot	General shop
G. Cutting	Greengrocer
W. Styles	Bootmaker
F.J. Bromley	Grocer
Mrs Townsend	Baker
James Helps	Greengrocer
Charles William Harvey	Bootmaker
Robert Freeman	Fishmonger
Mrs Talbot	General Shop
William H. Mead	Grocer
James Maunton	General shop
Charles W. Mead	General shop
Joseph Brand	General shop
Ferrigino Salvatoro	Shop
Joshuah Hance	Shoemaker
G. Tiegen	Grocer
C. Wilson	Greengrocery
John Sibbald	Shopkeeper
H.J. Gwyer	General Shop
J. Plumley	Confectioner
Miss Fitgerald	Grocer
Henry Gordon	Confectioner
Mrs Ofen	Grocer
Mrs Emma Charlwood	Confectioner
S.C. Teague	Grocer
W.J. Batch	Draper
Misses Izaard	Confectioners
R.E. Belsham	Grocer
Edward Charlwood	Confectioner
T.W. Grist	Confectioner
Mrs C. Tyler	Fishmonger
James Helps	Greengrocer

PUBLIC HOUSES
Proprietors 1855-1930

Joseph Chamberlain   Beer Retailer
John Ticehurst   Coffee Shop

'The Oxford Arms'
Oxford Road

Wm. Abnett
Henry Rabould
James William Bromley
Frederick Charles Russell
Clara Matilda Hurlock
William Butcher
Wm. J. Brown
Christopher Thomas Williams
Frederick Peter Gardner
Charles Vincent Giles
William Ewen
William Gough
Percy Victor Blackburn
R.E. Faircloth
Robert W. Collett
James Catt Snr.
James Catt Jnr.

'Fox under the Hill'
Eagle Hill

'The Eagle'
New Spa Road

Isaac Smith
Joshua Radburn
William Havden
Henry Dobbs

Shovelling snow outside the pub.

APPENDIX 9

CURRENCY	Imperial	Decimal	Colloquial expression
Farthing	$\frac{1}{4}$d		Fadger, tiddler
Halfpenny	$\frac{1}{2}$d		
Three farthings	$\frac{3}{4}$d		
One pence	1d	$\frac{1}{2}$p	Penny or copper
Two pence	2d	1p	
Three pence	3d		Originally a silver coin called 'Joey'
Six pence	6d	$2\frac{1}{2}$p	Tanner
One shilling	1/-	5p	Bob
Two shillings	2/-	10p	Two bob, etc.
Two shillings & sixpence	2/6d	$12\frac{1}{2}$p	Half a crown or half a dollar
Five shillings	5/-	25p	Crown or dollar
Ten shillings	10/-	50p	Half a nicker, half a quid
Twenty shillings	£1 0s.0d	100p	Nicker, quid
Twenty one shillings	£1 1s 0d	105p	Guinea

Norwood, Croydon, 1861.

PEOPLE PASSING THROUGH NEW TOWN

Abnett	Bloom	Catt	Curtis	Endersley
Abraham	Bollam	Ceresche	Cutting	Evans
Adams	Bollard	Cervitus	Cutts	Ewen
Acambar	Bore	Chamberlain		
Alexanders	Bowdary	Chambers	Dance	Fahney
Allards	Bowell	Chandler	Darling	Fairclough
Alley	Bower	Chapman	Dartnall	Fanner
Andrews	Boyle	Charles	Davenport	Farley
Anstiss	Bracklesham	Charlesworth	Davey	Fenner
Archer	Bran	Charwood	Davis	Fern
Armitstead	Bray	Childs	Davison	Finnin
ArnoldAslett	Bright	Chipping	Dawe	Fisher
Atkinson	Broderick	Chubb	Daws	Fogwell
Austin	Bromley	Church	Day	Foote
Avery	Brooks	Clanfield	Deacon	Ford
	Brown	Clapham	Dean	Fowler
Bailey	Bruce	Clappitt	Dee	Francis
Balchin	Bryan	Clard	Dench	Franks
Ball	Bryant	Clare	Denton	Freeman
Ballard	Budd	Clarence	Divall	French
Banks	Bugbird	Clark	Dobbs	Friend
Barlow	Bull	Clements	Doggett	Fuchia
Barnes	Bullen	Cloud	Dorrett	
Bartlett	Burchell	Collier	Dover	Gardner
Bates	Burgess	Collins	Downes	Garnham
Batt	Burgon	Connah	Drewitt	Garrotty
Beadle	Burrows	Conway	Dunham	Gearing
Beams	Burtenshaw	Coole	Dunicliffe	Geary
Beaton	Burton	Cooper	Dunk	Gee
Beatty	Bushel	Coppard	Dunn	Gent
Becketts	Butcher	Corgram	Durling	George
Beddle	Byford	Corliss	Dyke	Gereghty
Benrose		Corner		Gibbs
Berry	Caddick	Cornish	Earl	Giles
Biddle	Cadney	Court	Earlagh	Gill
Billings	Cahill	Cove	Early	Gillingham
Billington	Cambridge	Creasey	Eden	Gladfield
Birch	Camp	Cripps	Edwards	Glanfield
Bird	Carbutt	Crockett	Elliott	Godfrey
Black	Carpenter	Crook	Elmer	Goodman
Blackburn	Carter	Crouch	Elphic	Goodwin
Blackmore	Catham	Cummings	Embury	Gordon

Goreham
Gould
Graham
Grainger
Grange
Grant
Grayson
Green
Grimshaw
Guglimotte
Guires
Gusterson

Hackham
Haggarty
Hales
Hall
Hance
Harding
Harrington
Harris
Harrods
Harvey
Hayden
Head
Helps
Helsers
Hempstead
Henderson
Hewitts
Higham
Hill
Hillyer
Hoare
Hockham
Holder
Hollands
Holliday
Hollowell
Holman
Holness
Holton
Hook
Hooper
Horn
Houcher
Houghton
Howard

Howe
Hunnisett
Hunt
Hurlock
Hutchinson

Ingram
Inman
Ives
Izaard

Jackson
James
Jee
Jeffrey
Jingle
Johnson
Jones
Joyce

Kalaheshill
Keable
Kearns
Keiller
Kennedy
Kennell
Kent
Kettle
Keys
Kiddell
Killum
King
Kitchen
Kitchener
Knepper
Knight
Knivett
Kyrke

Lainick
Land
Lane
Langley
Langridge
Larby
Last
Latter
Lawrence

Leach
Leason
Lee
Leeks
Letts
Leversuch
Lewcock
Leyt
Lidbetter
Linden
Ling
Lomas
Longhurst
Lovejoy
Lucas
Lufter
Lynn

Macy
Mallett
Marchant
Margets
Markham
Marsh
Marshman
Martin
Masingham
Mason
Mates
Mathews
Mauri
May
Maynard
McIver
Mead
Meadows
Medland
Mencke
Miller
Mills
Mitticock
Moist
Money
Morgan
Morley
Morris
Morrison
Mountain

Moyler
Munday
Munnings
Murfell
Mussett

Nash
Neale
Newton
Nichols
Norman
Norris
North
Norwood

Oatey
Odle
Osbourne
Osson
O'Connor

Padon
Page
Palmer
Parrish
Payne
Percival
Perry
Philpots
Pickett
Pither
Pitt
Plumbridge
Poole
Powel
Price
Privet
Pymble

Quilter

Radburn
Radford
Randel
Ranger
Ranner
Raper
Raven

Rawson
Read
Reid
Rex
Reybold
Reynolds
Richards
Riddle
Roberts
Robinson
Rockingham
Romero
Romney
Ross
Russell

Salmon
Salvatoro
Samson
Sandford
Saunders
Sawyer
Scarborough
Scrimshaw
Searle
Self
Senior
Shave
Shepherd
Shoebridge
Sibbald
Silvester
Simmonds
Simon
Simpkins
Simpson
Sirex
Slater
Slater
Sleet
Smead
Smith
Snell
Soper
Sorrel &
    Talbot
Spain
Spurgeon

Squirrell	Sullivan	Tolley	Wade	Wiggins
Stanford		Tompkins	Waits	Williams
Starr	Tagg	Tooley	Wallace	Willis
Stead	Tappenden	Townley	Walshaw	Wills
Stent	Tasker	Townsend	Walton	Wilmot
Stephens	Taylor	Treadbetter	Warr	Wilsmore
Stevens	Terry	Treman	(Waugh)	Wilson
Stiles	Tester	Trice	Watson	Wood
Stockdale	Teston	Tripp	Webb	Woolhouse
Stocker	Thomas	Trowers	Wedge	Wooton
Stokes	Tidy	Turner	Wells	Wort
Stone	Ticehurst	Tyler	Westaway	Wren
Street	Tiegens		Westley	Wright
Stripe	Tilly	Upton	Wheatley	
Stripp	Tipping	Uwin	Whightman	
Style	Todd		Whitch	
Sucking	Tolgate	Vinall	Whitfield	

A tram outside the Crystal Palace.